MENTORED

A MANUAL FOR LEGACY LEADERSHIP

DAVID OGIDINTA

DEDICATION

I dedicate this book to God Almighty, the Master Mentor for entrusting us with this sacred duty of mentorship and helping us with the know-how to help others become better version of themselves.

ACKNOWLEDGEMENT

On behalf of everyone who has benefitted from mentorship, I want to thank all mentors for the great values they add to lives. You indeed must be proud of what you do.

Special thanks to my wife, Onyedikachi, for her endless support. Your continuous reminder and encouragement spurred me to complete this book after about 2 years of abandoning the work at an 80% level of completion.

I want to thank Dr Florence Ofovwe, my partner and the editor of a large part of this book. Your passion for the work of God, especially as it affects young people, is worthy of emulation. Let's continue to do more together.

Special thanks to Mr Sam of the Soul Fitness Centre, for sharing his great insights and agreeing to write the foreword for this book. I have watched you make a significant and transformational impact in the lives of many young people, including those who were headed towards self-destruction.

To those who shared their personal experiences free of charge to help others, you all have added great value to this book. Special thanks to Prof. Ezekiel CN, Sam Nwokomah, Soonest Nathaniel, Opeyemi Adeniyi, Dr Kolawole Ayeni, Stella Otuonye, Dr Muiz Akinyemi, Makanjuola Emmanuel and Oluwawapelumi Afolayan.

FOREWORD

Mentorship is a beautiful thing. It is the passing on of wisdom and experience from one generation to the next, the sharing of hard-won insights and lessons learned. It is an opportunity to guide and support someone as they navigate their path, to share in their triumphs and setbacks, and to help them become the best version of themselves.

Mentorship is more than the impartation of knowledge. It is also about building relationships, creating connections that transcend the superficial and delve into the deeper aspects of what it means to be a human. It is about supporting and encouraging someone to grow and develop in ways they may never have imagined.

In this book, "Mentored: A Manual for Legacy Leadership", David C. Ogidinta, deliberately and intentionally, serves a full recipe of mentorship in all its forms. It is a tribute to the mentors who have shaped our lives and a guide for those who seek to pay it forward. Whether you are an experienced mentor looking to deepen your practice or someone just starting on your mentorship journey, this book is for you. It is also highly recommended for every young person, student, entrepreneur and those starting or looking to boost their career. A journey with a clear pathway will suffer fewer hitches.

So let us dive in and explore the wonderful world of mentorship. Let us share stories and insights, and let us be inspired by the powerful impact of mentorship in our world.

Sam. Nwaokomah

Mentor Extraordinaire & Founder, Soul Fitness Centre, a Non-Government Organization and a Direct Youth Intervention Program geared at influencing young people and society through programs in guidance, counselling, friendship and role modelling.

Abuja, Nigeria.

INTRODUCTION

One of the most sacred tasks given to man is to look after his fellow human being. This is hard and requires continuous renewal of skills because man is the most dynamically sophisticated entity in existence. However, the harder the job of a mentor, parent or leader, the greater the joy that follows when the job is well done. The excitement a mentor feels when his protégé succeed is the same as when a successful athlete wins a trophy. Life makes the most meaning when you give life to another. When mentorship is however denied, neglected, or poorly executed, the result could only be imagined. As Jim Rhon has advised, "Don't let your learning lead to knowledge, you will become a fool; let your learning lead to action, you will become wealthy".

I have had an exciting and rewarding mentorship career so far with over two (2) decades of experience; impacting thousands of young people from different socio-cultural backgrounds, faith, and career interests. I desire to contribute this to the body of knowledge through this manual. I consider it a legacy that will benefit both old and upcoming mentors; and for new career babes to know their need for a mentor, and how or where they can be found. It will also serve as an accountability guide. One of the greatest lessons I have learned during my career is that the moment you decide you want something better for yourself, the universe begins to align in your favour. You must get tired of an average life! When you get to this point, a new you will emerge and you can either nurture it to be phenomenal or remain the same.

My dream as a child was to be a medical missionary and I pursued it. I started a Bachelor of Science degree programme in Microbiology from Babcock University, but just before my graduation, the prospect of becoming a medical doctor became vague. This was caused by hardship and my new interest to reach a larger audience at once rather than being restricted to the bench or attending to only one patient at a time as a clinician. I soon realized that what I needed was a mentor to help me understand the scope of my dream and the better ways I can achieve it.

In 2010, I met Dr Laz Udu Eze as a friend who later became my mentor. He was a senior Corps member in my Community Development Service (CDS) group, HIV/AIDS CDS Group, Abuja Chapter. Our interests aligned quickly. Since he was a medical doctor, there were a lot of things I could learn from him. A few years after NYSC, he travelled abroad to complete his Master's degree program in Public Health, a choice that partly inspired me to do the same. I recall our first conversation when I intimated to him about my interest to pursue a Master's degree in Public Health. He didn't hesitate to give me his blessings and guidance in the most possible way.

This exposure helped put me on the right track to achieving my childhood dream. I now volunteer my skills, time, and resources to support public health organizations both locally and internationally. In 2019, Dr Laz personally recruited and directly supervised my work as a Resource Mobilization Officer (South-South Nigeria) for Pink Oak, a foundation that sponsored the treatment and care for Cancer patients in Nigeria where he served as the Executive Director. Through his mentorship, I was awarded the "Most Outstanding Volunteer in 2019".

This book promises to expose you to what I consider a successful mentorship relationship and serve as a guide to legacy leadership. It is divided into eight (8) chapters; each chapter represents a letter from the word 'MENTORED', which is also the book title. You are about to discover the dos and don'ts in mentorship, how to or not encourage, rudiments of nurturing, expected outcomes of transformation, optimism and reassurances, entrusted legacy and determination for success. It is written in simple English with relatable stories for easy assimilation and bullet points for easy retention. It is also not too bulky.

There is the icing on the cake. I have a list of amazing personalities from different works of life who accepted to share their transformation stories resulting from mentorship. The entries are from Nigeria, South Africa, Austria, Canada, the USA, and the United Kingdom. You will find them valuable in improving your mentorship experience. Another reason for this addition is to immortalize our selfless mentors who knowingly or otherwise became the right pedestal for us to achieve our goals, as well as to mentees for accepting to partner with their mentors, ready to pay it forward.

I wish you a good reading experience. Congratulations!

CHAPTER ONE

MENTORED

Knowledge is power. You can only feel this power when you put the knowledge to use. As there is knowledge on one hand, there is 'putting to use' and the power that follows on the other hand. We have all seen both the young and old wield certain powers to achieve their set goals but those who had little help on their path to success seem to achieve more. Mentorship is simply the transfer of knowledge and experiences from one more knowledgeable or experienced (mentor) to another with little or no knowledge or experience but desirous of guidance to achieve set goals (mentee).

Does society need mentors? Would I achieve more if I have someone willing to guide me through my aspirations? Is there anyone who understands my dreams, and who may wish to help me attain them? Is there anything I can do to help someone else achieve their goals?

The importance of mentorship in a growing society can never be overemphasized. When you understand what needs to be done, it becomes effortless. Parents are part of the greatest mentors of all time. They may not transfer major vocational skills, but without the right guidance from parents, children turn out worse than what society expects. Parents lay a solid foundation that is simply improved upon by other mentors such as teachers in schools and other career/vocational masters. It is expected that in the course of this book, mentors will appreciate the need to consciously teach, guide, direct, promote, expose and monitor the progress of their mentees to achieve the desired results. The following categories try to inexhaustibly place mentors into various groups. Where do you belong and what role do you currently play?

Primary mentors: Parents, siblings/close relations, and friends.

Secondary mentors: School teachers, religious teachers, etc.

Tertiary mentors: Chosen career/vocational influencers.

Quaternary mentors: Indirect influencers like politicians, society heroes or villains.

WHY MENTOR?

Mentorship, at its core, guarantees young people that someone cares about them, assures them that they are not alone in dealing with day-to-day challenges, and makes them feel like they matter. Studies confirm that quality mentorship relationships have powerful positive effects on young people in a variety of personal, academic and professional situations. Ultimately, mentorship connects a young person to personal growth and development, including social and economic opportunities, yet a large number of people grow up without this critical asset.

Effective mentorship plays an important role in professional growth and development, as well as in the academic success of any mentee. Excellent mentors provide a distinct vision and guide their mentees to achieve the goals inspired by these visions. Several works of literature reveal definitive characteristics that show that a successful mentorship relationship can enhance productivity, efficiency and motivation. Successful mentors take mentees under their wings for guidance, inspiration, and encouragement and in the process, they create motivated, productive, and successful protégés, thereby leaving a legacy.

Transfer of knowledge and the difficulties in developing critical thinking skills and independent learning are very serious business. According to Katherine Schrubbe, while trying to analyze what made the difference in her 2 years dental education career, she claimed "I now have the guidance and dedication of an encouraging and inspiring mentor"[1]. Many people tell stories of how others influenced a major change in their lives; this refers to individual mentors. According to Harvard Business Review 1978, 'Everyone who makes it has a mentor'.[2] These people claim that a major factor in their success as individuals is having mentors. Mentors can inspire confidence in others, push them to their limits, and continue to develop them to their greatest potential.

It is easy to think that you don't need anyone, or claim that whatever you have is a product of hard work and thus, assert to be a lone ranger. But I've grown to realize that we all are products of other people's input, support, guidance, criticism and mentorship. I am a product of a complex mix of ideas and I pride myself as one with a very holistic positive outlook on life because of my contributors.

The following are a few individuals who have affected my personal life and career development in great measure at different times:

Prof Chimezie Omeonu

Elder Eirdy Abraham

Dr/Mrs Florence Ofovwe

Dr Laz Udu Eze

Mr Blessing Egbele

Goldsmith et al3 in their publication identified a few great qualities of mentors that make them indispensable.

Mentors are people who can see more in you than you see in yourself.

They create vision and development plans that take advantage of your strengths, abilities and potential for growth.

Effective mentors are so unshakably convinced that we have greatness in us, and their vision of what is possible is so clear and powerful, that they wind up convincing us too.

Here are a few of what mentors achieve in their mentees when effective mentorship takes place. Adapted from 'The Road to Success with a Mentor' by Gordon4

Independence.

Self-confidence.

Job satisfaction.

Upward mobility.

Decision-making/problem-solving skills.

High network of professionals in the mentee's chosen career path.

DANGERS OF NOT HAVING MENTORS

When you talk about mentorship in the Bible, one good example that comes to mind is Samuel in 1 Samuel 1 & 2. Hannah, who didn't have a child, thought of having one that will be useful and will add value. When she prayed and God gave her Samuel, she believed that she cannot raise a child who will not turn out well, or come to fulfil destiny or the purpose of his existence. So she chose Eli. Eli if you recall, was a renowned priest and the first to lead at a critical time in their nation's history. If you have a child or anyone who looks up to you for the plans for their future; who will you lead them to? Will you model them after the crazy musicians, corrupt politicians or some dubious businessmen or women of the present world or after mundane things? Hannah made a great choice, and that choice is nothing but to help plan for the future and life of her son, Samuel. Even when Eli's family was breaking down, the foundation that he had laid for Samuel above his children came to play. God needed to send a message to Eli's family and he chose Samuel based on the training he had got, consequent on the best choice of Hannah.

Compare Samuel with the biological children of Eli. Samuel had a protected and successful future laid out by Eli the mentor, whereas Hophni and Phinehas who ought to take over from their father ruined their lives for lack of mentorship. This might not be the right time to talk about whose fault it was for their failures but simply to show the effect of lack of mentorship. They were so corrupt; God couldn't stand their continuous rebellion and their father's complacency even though he had served dutifully as a great mentor for someone else. Imagine if Samuel was not mentored in the things of God, he would fall off as well. You can choose whom your children or wards must associate with. Mentorship is not for children alone; adults can begin to model their lives after something great, someone great, or something bigger and better. We learn and grow by example, so when we make the right choice of what this example should be, we have secured a better future.

For young professionals or entrepreneurs, it is good to want to create something on your own. However, while you might have a great idea, you may not know what you should be doing with it, and at which time to develop it into a suitable business. The dangers or implications of not having good mentors can only be imagined.

It will be difficult to grow as fast as competitors with mentors.

You have no one's mistake to learn from except yours.

Poor leadership skills.

You are limited to space, time, and resources within your reach.

Lack of accountability partner.

You are at risk of quitting early.

WHO INITIATES THE MENTORSHIP RELATIONSHIP: MENTORS OR MENTEES?

It is widely perceived that a mentorship relationship focuses primarily on the mentors and their role in initiating a relationship. However, the role of the mentee in establishing this relationship is equally critical. It is expected of a mentee to attract a good mentor since it is believed that he gains the most. Mentors want to associate with winners, with rising stars, so that some of the stardust will brush off on them5. We can agree that this relationship ought to be mutually beneficial.

In my relationship with Dr Omeonu, I simply made myself visible. In the early 2000s during the occasion of his father's death, he came home to receive visitors. He stood out as the only educated person in my community at that time and he has achieved so much for himself and his family to my admiration. I had completed my secondary school education and was passionate about pursuing a university degree. I decided to write a letter of condolence to him while expressing my intention to meet and discuss my future ambitions. He graciously obliged.

The mentee should therefore exhibit certain characteristics that will attract a good mentor; willingness to take on responsibilities, receptive to feedback, self-perceived growth potential, self-motivated, ability to perform in multiple skilled areas, history of seeking new and challenging assignments, demonstrates teachable skills, ambitious and ready to do what it takes.

An effective mentorship relationship evolves from a natural affinity between two individuals. They begin to interact informally after they must have worked together for a while and developed mutual respect1. A certain level of attraction must exist for an appropriate interpersonal match between mentors and their mentees. Talent draws the mentor to the mentee while accomplishment and power draw the mentee to the mentor.

Fawcett reports that effective mentors possess patience, enthusiasm, knowledge, sense of humour and exhibit respect for others. Mentors should serve as advocates for the protégé and get to know him/her, thus allowing the protégé succeed and the mentor-learner relationship to grow7. The mentorship pair must critically possess compatible personalities and common professional interests.

A mentor-protégé pair that works well together and complements one another is critical to the success of both individuals. When this is right, the mentee will experience many positive outcomes from the mentorship exercise.

If many young professionals welcome the guidance of accomplished mentors, the benefits may be immeasurable.

Lack of proper mentorship, and adequate mentors in most professions, create a huge deficit for certain professionals because the elders don't mentor the young ones or the young ones are not willing to do what it takes to succeed. Whichever is the case, a good mentorship experience will change the narrative.

In the cultivation of the mentor-protégé relationship, a close working status may exist that allows for daily contact between the mentorship pair, bestowing special status on the protégé by association with the senior mentor and access to an inner circle. The work of the protégé may take on a special significance that enhances the career of both the protégé and mentor, and as the relationship develops, the mentor may cultivate the protégé's leadership and ability through example, opportunities of practice or direction9.

According to Stone, additional encouragement and instruction that protégés receive from mentors can motivate them to work harder, face challenging assignments, and operate outside their boxes; resulting in increased productivity10. There are lots of goals young professionals would venture into if they are certain of the backing and support of successful mentors.

The beautiful thing about effective mentorship is that while it is a cumbersome task, there are positive outcomes for everyone involved. The growth of the mentees towards independence and the satisfaction of the mentor in his protégé's accomplishment are intertwined. One successful mentorship exercise inspires the beginning of another.

Mentorship is a lifelong process. Each of us has the potential to mentor another; it is now our duty to promote the role of a mentor and to do it more consciously. Some people consistently influence our lives in various ways. If you think about it, they mentored us in ways we can't fully recall. Some say that mentorship maintains a tradition: a knowledge or information process whereby the mentor provides a base for the protégé, passing on or handing down the tradition of inquiry, and sharing how to acquire critical information11.

The value of having the guidance of an intelligent, dedicated, encouraging and genuine mentor can never be overemphasized. And we all must agree that effective mentorship is critical for success. But mentorship is not a skill that comes naturally to everyone, hence the need for the thoughts shared in this book. I have observed that we have few mentors because those who ought to assume this position were not mentored themselves, so they lack the know-how on effective mentorship.

According to W. Brad Johnson, a Professor of Psychology at the US Naval Academy and author of books and journal articles on mentorship, "good mentoring shapes not only the current generation but future generations as well".

CHAPTER TWO

ENCOURAGED

"A word of encouragement during a failure is worth more than praises after success" -Anonymous

A mentor offers wisdom and encouragement to a mentee. Based on their personal experience, they can provide unique insights into situations that the mentee may otherwise not consider. A good mentor builds up mentees and helps them become the best version of themselves.

You may not assume the role of a mentor, but a word of encouragement might be enough for someone to stay on course and eventually achieve their goals. On every adventure, we all get tired or confused and might need someone to give us a simple push, not in terms of money, connections, or specialized training, but with a word of hope. This will go a long way in spurring your beneficiary to greatness.

Throughout history, we have inspired men and women who achieved amazing feats through the support and encouragement of other mentors. We often look at mentorship as very cumbersome and demanding, but giving words of encouragement costs nothing. "Well done", "you are smart", "you are on the right track", "don't give up", "you are capable of great things", "you are just a few steps away from greatness", etc., might be the right word someone desperately needs. You do not need to be a celebrated mentor, pastor, leader, philanthropist or accomplished politician to encourage. People in business, athletes, academicians, politicians, etc. – everyone can be inspired by a mentor.

It is widely believed that the mentee leads the mentorship relationship. It is usually of their own volition to seek out a mentor. However, both the mentor and mentee work together to achieve the goal of the mentee. Most mentees are just in need of someone to encourage them, demand accountability and motivate them to do their best.

Mentoring is part of everyone's life, whether they recognize it or not. Informal mentorship takes place throughout one's life and part of the goal of this book is to make readers become conscious of this role and be able to discharge it effectively. To mentor effectively, the focus should not only be on the mentee's successes; failures and opportunities to improve should be discussed as well. Good mentors know how to talk to and encourage their protégé. Resilience is an important quality in any line of work and mentees should be taught to develop that. It is also important to remember that no matter who you are or where you work, there is always an opportunity to mentor others.

WHY DO PEOPLE NEED ENCOURAGEMENT

Words are so powerful but we often underestimate their potential. They can create and destroy. They are capable of charting a new course in one's life. The words you speak can offer encouragement to another person or may send them further into despair. Hence, we must choose our words carefully. 1 Thessalonians 5 vs 11 says, "Therefore encourage one another and build each other up, just as you are doing". Encouraging words build lives; and as we encourage others, we equally benefit. People who encourage others, find it easier to show gratitude, feel joy and achieve success.

Without encouragement, we can only imagine what our lives and career will be like;

Both our personal and professional lives will feel pointless and cumbersome.

We will be overwhelmed by the pains of our lives and careers.

We might feel unloved or unappreciated.

We may begin to think that God is a liar or unconcern about our welfare.

We may feel lonely and begin to doubt if we are capable of success.

While everyone wants to succeed and achieve their goals, many need a little push. A lot of us go through phases where we feel stuck or weighed down; at that point, we would love to talk to someone who will tell us that everything will be okay. It is nice to be there for someone when they need you the most.

It will, in turn, motivate you.

It will help in changing the world.

You will make genuine friends.

You will be helping others.

You can change the way people react to constructive criticism.

It will make you see others differently.

It may open up a plethora of opportunities for you.

It is said that no one is an island; even islands are bordered by water bodies. Your encouragement can be a bridge for someone to navigate their path to success and in the end, you will be happy you did.

HOW TO GIVE ENCOURAGEMENT

"Too often we underestimate the power of a touch, a smile, a kind word, a listening ear, an honest compliment, or the smallest act of caring, all of which have the potential to turn a life around." – Leo Buscaglia

Many of the world's greatest achievements began with empowering words of encouragement from a friend, partner, parent, teacher or mentor. When someone is feeling insecure, unsure, or apprehensive about taking constructive action or pursuing favourable opportunities, you should convey to them your belief that they are capable of great feats and that their efforts are worthwhile. Having an opportunity to offer encouragement to another person is a privilege. The consequence of your unselfishness is that you will feel happier and better about yourself. Encouragement doesn't take much time or effort from you, but it could mean the world to a person who is swimming against the tides of trouble.

Follow these few steps while encouraging:

1.   Recognize the person's struggle: When giving words of encouragement, the first thing is to determine the level of difficulty. Do not pretend to know what they are going through or need until they let you in. Generalizing or suggesting that they can 'work it out' is less helpful than specifically addressing the issue that is holding them back. This way, you show empathy.

2.   Be positive: If you want them to be more at ease with the prospect of doing something, you should indicate confidence in their abilities and focus on what can be

accomplished and what potential benefits may be reaped by boldly taking action. Remind them of their previous accomplishments and what they gained because of their efforts. Encourage them to believe that their dreams are achievable, and offer steps to make them easier.

3.   Be sincere: Encouragement is most effective when you say things that you mean. Undue flattery may produce unrealistic expectations and ultimately cause more harm than good. Honestly expressing your desire for their success and your expectation that the experience will be good for them can help motivate them to take action. You can share a personal story relevant to your mentee or anyone you need to encourage at that time.

4.   Inspire a healthy outlook: Assure them that their worth is not determined by the outcome of any given endeavour. Everyone experiences both success and failure at different points throughout life; it is important to learn from both. Let them know that the current phase will end as soon as they learn the lessons and follow through. Dreams do not end until they are achieved; so charge them to focus on the goal until it is achieved.

5.   Offer to do more: Be willing to follow up with your mentees beyond verbal rhetoric. Rather than just encouraging, teach them the process and as much as you can, show them how it is done. This way, you build their confidence and whenever you are not there, they will be able

to handle themselves well. Samuel heard God's voice but couldn't figure out where it was coming from until Eli taught him how to answer such calls; he would have continued to go back and forth.

6. Be realistic: You must set a realistic expectations of the efforts and strategies you have deployed to help your mentee. Everything might not work out as you expect, so lay out your words carefully and don't be forceful if it doesn't go your way.

WAYS OF ENCOURAGING OTHERS

There are many ways that we can give people hope and one of the easiest is to encourage them regularly. That may sound vague or unimportant, but encouragement is emotionally equivalent to throwing a rope at a drowning man. Hope is empowering and since encouragement gives hope, you can help to empower someone who is hurting.

Here is a list of some easy and practical ways that you can encourage people adapted from Sherry Ritter's "24 Ways to Encourage Others"

Go to lunch or dinner together.

Praise the person publicly.

Offer to do a task for the person.

Spend time listening to the person talk.

Ask how you can be of help to them.

Offer to babysit their children so they can get away for a while.

Call the person often just to let them know you were thinking of them.

Post a compliment or encouraging words on their Facebook wall.

When someone is making changes in their life, notice it and offer words of praise.

Smile as you pass by others. You never know who needs to see a kind face to give them hope.

Write a letter of commendation to the person's boss.

Write a note and put it in their lunch box or leave the note on their desk.

Give them a gift.

Hug the person.

Give them compliments.

Give the person an uplifting card.

Give the person a motivational book.

Give the person a gift card to a restaurant.

Send chocolates.

Send the person flowers.

Tell the person a funny joke.

Tell the person that you love them.

Tell the person you will pray for them.

Tell the person that you appreciate them.

WHO SHOULD ENCOURAGE?

The word 'encouragement' in the context of this book should be everybody's business, to achieve continuous and sustainable mentorship. However, much more is expected from the government in the way of policies and programs, family, friends, social, religious and academic institutions, and, existing mentors.

Government

Nigeria, and indeed Africa's resource and potential competitive advantage in the global economy is its young and growing workforce. Young people make up the highest percentage of our population and this growing society needs an active, high-powered network of mentors and programs to drive their aspirations. Young people need skills that will enable them to secure their future. Entrepreneurs need access to opportunities, skill training, and capital to grow their businesses, create employment and grow the economy; and young people need access to reliable and affordable financial services and products.

There are several youth empowerment programs in Nigeria, some of which are organized by individuals, private organizations or the government to develop the Nigerian youths. This is a way of encouraging youths in society, to show that they are important and appreciated. However, more programs should be organized and the existing ones should be well publicized and made accessible so that more people can take advantage of them. The following are a few of the benefits of government programs or policies targeted to encourage young people:

They create avenues for the development of new potential.

They equip the youth for the tasks ahead.

They develop entrepreneurial skills.

They create a pool of relevant skills to solve targeted problems in society.

They reduce dependence on the government, thereby reducing pressure on the economy.

They are a veritable way to check youth restiveness.

They promote global competitiveness.

Rather than brand the youths as lazy, the government should make a strong statement and invest in supporting its youths in different vocations, and create awareness to encourage their skills while exploring new opportunities.

Family

"In the family, happiness is in the ratio in which each is serving the others." – Henry Ward Beecher

Family is a critical part of society and there's nothing wrong with helping your children, parents, and other loved ones in a financial bind.

It is said that family support is the most significant factor towards one's success. As the family is the first learning place, it is also one of the most vital support systems that make people successful. Family teaches the crucial fundamentals of life and guides personal values and social behaviours. Most importantly, whether you are at the top or bottom in your personal life or profession, the family is always there to fall back on. These qualities are assumed to be the norm if all things are equal but sometimes the case is different. I encourage the family to play its essential role as a mentorship unit.

Healthy families respect each other, hold individual members accountable for their behaviours, and are supportive in times of need. All family members need to be held accountable for what they say they will and won't do. Building a strong family include being able to rely on others, but that will be thwarted when someone does not come through. In addition, it is important to support family members when they are struggling. Helping them through tough times will give your family that bond it needs.

Here are some important factors of a family as a support system, and where they are lacking, they need to be developed and strengthened.

Family;

gives you a sense of belonging.

loves you in ways that no one can.

helps you make decisions.

protects and comforts you.

keep you entertained.

enable you to grow and learn.

celebrate all your wins.

help you pull through failures and make sure you are never lonely.

prays for you.

ensures that you are connected to the resources you need to succeed.

is reliable.

There is a need to do some soul-searching as a member of a family. From the list above, rate yourself and see how you can improve to be the best help or mentor your relations get.

Existing Mentors

Mentorship is a relationship between two people with the goal of professional and personal development in view. The mentor is usually an experienced individual who shares knowledge, experience, and advice with a less experienced person called a mentee. This relationship, among many others, encourages the mentee to be the best he/she can be and the mentor is usually passionate to see his protégé succeed. Sadly, although many mentees feel like their mentors satisfy all of these basic mentorship needs, they may still be lacking in encouragement. If you want to be the best mentor, coach, or leader, you need to master the act of encouraging your mentee. There are multiple ways to encourage your mentee and here are a few:

Encourage your mentee to set attainable goals.

Keep your mentees in mind for various opportunities.

Show them care through your actions.

Be ready to refer them to other professionals and resources, and insist on feedback.

Be willing to make sacrifices that will bring your mentees closer to achieving their set goals.

It is good to note that mentoring partnerships can be mutually beneficial and rewarding, on both professional and personal levels. Mentors can develop leadership skills and gain a personal sense of satisfaction from knowing that they've helped someone. Meanwhile, mentees can expand their knowledge and skills, gain valuable advice from more experienced persons, and build their professional networks. Both partners can improve their communication skills, learn new ways of thinking, and, ultimately, advance their careers.

Mentorship relationships can be mutual, or two-way, with one person being the mentor and the other, the mentee. It can also be one-way, whereby an individual may have his or her mentor while acting as a mentor for another person at the same time13.

Academic Institutions

The changing landscape in institutions of learning has made it difficult for less experienced colleagues to find persons willing to invest in, and support their professional development. According to Daloz, mentorship is an important development activity that can have a positive influence on the growth and professional development of those involved in the mentorship relationship, but more so on the person being mentored14. The mentor here serves the following roles, adapted from15;

An advisor who assists the mentee in setting and attaining career goals.

A strategist for networking and building relationships that will sustain a successful academic career.

An advocate for scholarly values and academic integrity.

Adept at resolving difficult work-related issues.

Able to provide constructive guidance and practical feedback.

Sensitive to the challenges of creating a work-life balance.

Prepared to make a reasonable time commitment.

Responsive to professional issues associated with identity including gender, race/ ethnicity, class, and sexual orientation.

Religious Organizations

God commanded that his people encourage each other because He knows we will need it. In the gospel of John, Jesus warned that "In this world, you will have trouble", after which He added a much-needed encouragement: "But take heart; I have overcome the world" (John 16:33). When encouragement is absent in the church, people will feel unloved, unimportant, useless, and forgotten. God knows His people need grace-filled reminders, so He calls us to encourage each other every day until His Son returns (Heb. 3:13). Everyone in your congregation needs to be encouraged, from the clergy to the laity, men and women, young and old. This should be an index for the growth of a loving and prosperous group.

According to Garrett Kell[16], strive to develop yourself to be a good encouragement to others:

Pray for God to make you an encourager.

Study the life of Barnabas and ask God to make you like him (Acts 4:36).

Make encouragement a daily discipline.

Pray for God to show you whom to encourage.

Use the scriptures if you're able.

Encourage your pastor regularly.

Pray that God would create a culture of encouragement in your church.

Be wise.

Get started.

Other authors and famous people have shared their thoughts about the importance of encouragement, and here are a few:

1. "The only person you are destined to become is the person you decide to be." - Ralph Waldo Emerson

2. "Start where you are. Use what you have. Do what you can." -Arthur Ashe

3. "How wonderful it is that nobody need wait a single moment before starting to improve the world." - Anne Frank

4. "When one door closes another door opens; but we so often look so long and so regretfully upon the closed door,

that we do not see the ones which open for us." - Alexander Graham Bell

5. "Life is a succession of lessons which must be lived to be understood."- Helen Keller

6. "When you get into a tight place and everything goes against you, till it seems as though you could not hang on a minute longer, never give up then, for that is just the place and time that the tide will turn." - Harriet Beecher Stowe

7. "You must do the thing you think you cannot do." - Eleanor Roosevelt

8. "If you don't pay appropriate attention to what has your attention, it will take more of your attention than it deserves." - David Allen

9. "I find hope in the darkest of days, and focus in the brightest. I do not judge the universe." - Dalai Lama

10. "Character cannot be developed in ease and quiet. Only through experience of trial and suffering can the soul be strengthened, ambition inspired, and success achieved." - Helen Keller

11. "It is by going down into the abyss that we recover the treasures of life. Where you stumble, there lies your treasure." - Joseph Campbell

12. "In essence, if we want to direct our lives, we must take control of our consistent actions. It's not what we do once in a while that shapes our lives, but what we do consistently." - Tony Robbins

13. "Our greatest weakness lies in giving up. The most certain way to succeed is always to try just one more time." - Thomas A. Edison

14. "You are never too old to set another goal or to dream a new dream." - C.S. Lewis

15. "Even if you fall on your face, you're still moving forward." - Victor Kiam

16. "Be miserable. Or motivate yourself. Whatever has to be done, it's always your choice." - Wayne Dyer

17. "Learn from the past, set vivid, detailed goals for the future, and live in the moment over which you have any control: now." - Denis Waitley

18. "Do you want to know who you are? Don't ask. Act! Action will delineate and define you." - Thomas Jefferson

19. "The key is to keep company only with people who uplift you, whose presence calls forth your best." - Epictetus

20. "Be impeccable with your word. Speak with integrity. Say only what you mean. Avoid using the word to speak against

yourself or to gossip about others. Use the power of your word in the direction of truth and love." - Miguel Angel Ruiz

21. "Act as if what you do makes a difference. It does." - William James

22. "Learning is the beginning of wealth. Learning is the beginning of health. Learning is the beginning of spirituality. Searching and learning is where the miracle process all begins." - Jim Rohn

23. "I'd rather attempt to do something great and fail than to attempt to do nothing and succeed." - Robert H. Schuller

24. "If it is the bread that you seek, you will have bread. If it is the soul you seek, you will find the soul. If you understand this secret, you know you are that which you seek." - Rumi

25. "Hang on; hold fast; the best is yet to come" - Florence Ofovwe.

CHAPTER THREE

NURTURED

Our society today needs intelligent and creative people more than ever. In this current situation, creativity is one of the most important lessons we can gain from great mentors whose duty is to nurture and transform their protégés into 'solution bearers'. Learning is a critical part of development; where knowledge and skills are acquired, they give rise to new and advanced behaviours. A mentor facilitates the nurturing process that leads to growth. It is a process of guidance, with the aim of behavioural modifications such that the mentee functions more effectively. Creating possibilities and providing guidance and support to others requires trust. It includes facilitating, bringing vision to life, and, enabling personal growth to take place.

For protégés, the mentorship relationship is not just about landing your next big job. To the mentors, there are many benefits in it for you also. Mentorship can be an enormously valuable experience for aspiring and established business leaders alike. Working with supportive, more experienced colleagues can help you develop the best version of yourself. Guiding a colleague, a child or any of your protégés toward their full potential can help you hone your coaching skills while shaping the next generation of leaders.

Nurturing is a big challenge, but when effectively done, its benefits cannot be overemphasized. Why do you think some plants grow and blossom more than others? When you think about what makes certain persons better than others, what makes some professionals excel beyond their peers; you will find a mentor who takes time to guide their protégés daily or routinely; brushing, clearing, tendering, and pruning them. One major thing about mentoring or nurturing is the intention, the consciousness that you are doing the job. In nature, however, things are expected to have a certain outcome. When a mango fruit falls and decays, rain makes it germinates, it grows into a tree and for many generations, this cycle continues. Nurturing, however, does not happen in isolation; it exists among individuals, groups or organizations. When someone points to a mentor that they are excited about, you will see that such a mentor must have put in a lot of work to ensure that the protégé has achieved what they had set out to achieve. And as we advocate in this book, the protégé grows to become a mentor himself to sustain continuous development.

Who should be nurtured?

Who should do the nurturing?

How does effective nurturing takes place?

When does nurturing begin or end?

Think about this concept and try to distinguish products of nature and nurture; think of the difference that could be made. I have learned that life is full of activities that often depend on inputs from others before they can truly exist.

BIBLICAL EXAMPLES OF NURTURE

There are good examples of nurturing experiences from the Bible. We learn numerous lessons on who, how and when to nurture, as well as many other factors that take part in this great process.

MOSES

Moses was born at a very important time in the history of his people. His destiny could have been cut short if not for the intervention of the Hebrew midwives who refused to kill the Hebrew male children as instructed by Pharaoh during the time of Moses's birth. Rather than killing him, his parents dropped him at the riverside where Pharaoh's daughter bathes. In nurturing Moses, different individuals played very important roles:

His Parents: Parents play a significant role in the choice of who, where and the things that contribute to shaping their children's life. Moses's parents, aware of their circumstance – the threat to their son's survival and their hope of a better life for him – decided to choose the right drop-off point, who should take up the responsibility of nurturing him and what they desire him to become in life.

These considerations are very important and parents must be conscious in choosing what will affect their children's lives, either now or in the future. Mistakes at this stage bear dire consequences upon the children, and the parents are equally the first to suffer the consequence of wrong choices. The choice of key players in the life of our children should not be left in the hands of others.

His Sister (Miriam): Family support is a critical factor in people's success. Choosing whom to guide our children and wards is not enough. We must monitor them to ensure they are doing a good job. Miriam was stationed close to the riverside where Moses was placed to ensure the right person pick up the lad, and she was ready to offer further assistance in the way of helpful suggestions. She said: "Shall I go and call a nurse for you from the Hebrew women, that she may nurse the child for you?" – Exodus 2 vs 7.

We find parents who neither know where their children's schools are nor who their teachers or coaches are. This is not to be encouraged. No matter the 'perfect' plan you have made for your children's education, find time to follow up so that they won't slip off your hand. Miriam would have revolted if the maids of Pharaoh's daughter had kept Moses for themselves. To her, the mission is successful and complete only when he gets to the right person, who, in this case, is Pharaoh's daughter.

The Nurturer (Moses's mother): Moses's mother came highly recommended and accepted by all interested parties to do a great job of nurturing the lad. She possessed all the requisite qualifications, years of experience and enthusiasm for the job. The people we hand off our children to must be of trusted character and knowledge that can drive our expectations for them. Who is your child's teacher or coach? Sometimes, parents make the mistake of allowing people of questionable character to have access to their children at an early stage. Their influence on the kids may eventually distort their values and put them off-track.

In choosing whom to nurture our kids and wards, you must consider putting round pegs into round holes. No one would hire a carpenter to do the job of a plumber. There were many women at the time, but none could fulfil God's plan for Moses's upbringing better than his mother. Of course, what God feels about who takes care of our children matter so much that it should not be ignored.

SAMUEL

Hannah recognized that God is the giver of children and can take care of them better than any parent, teacher or guardian could.

Similar to the case of Moses, Hannah chose to hand over the upbringing of Samuel to Eli. Both parents considered the future of their children in choosing who nurtures them. For Moses, perhaps the parents considered the possibility of him becoming the next Pharaoh in Egypt, hence they planted him on Pharaoh's daughter through whom they were certain this dream may be achieved. Whereas in the case of Samuel, Hannah hoped the lad may be the next high priest and she chose Eli, the only high priest at the time to nurture Samuel.

IMPORTANT SKILLS FOR EFFECTIVE NURTURING EXERCISE

Every educational system, through planning and production of specific curricula, tries to transfer different kinds of knowledge and skills to learners, preparing them to undertake their roles and responsibilities in real life. Just like other aspects of effective mentorship, to successfully nurture our protégés, mentors must possess certain skills.

1. The ability to identify talents in our mentees: The most attractive thing about mentees is their talents. The gardener takes his time to nurture a plant because he knows its potential if it receives the right nourishment. It may seem obvious, but simply believing that people have talent and potential, changes how we interact with them. With such an attitude, we are likely to convey confidence and positive expectations. Our language shifts towards opportunity and success. When we see talents we can work with, we communicate with them in various ways. However, the opposite is equally true. When you fail to see any talent to work with, it will be impossible to make headway.

2. Set mutually understood goals: Before entering into a nurturing relationship, there is a need to communicate the

goals of the relationship, so that both of you will be on the same page with clear expectations. The goal might be to help the mentee get promoted, secure funding, resolve performance issues, improve communication skills, etc. It is recommended that the mentee's goals take precedence. The mentee should be the person driving the schedule and the discussion topics. At each meeting, the mentee should bring a list of topics for discussion. They should brief their mentor on the topic, present the problem/challenge/opportunity, outline their current thoughts about the strategies or next steps, and solicit their mentor's advice. If the goals don't align, there will be confusion. This will reveal selfishness and result in mutual suspicion.

3. You must create opportunities to develop the talents: Nurturing takes time and sacrifice. We need to be ready to reschedule some activities that are important to us for others to gain experience and skills. This step can be difficult for some, because we may think we are the only ones who can do it right or because we need to be at the centre of attention. We should give room for small failures to occur while staying close enough to help them pick up the pieces and learn from the experience. Developing talent requires that we delegate and still provide the support that leads to growth.

4. Listen, teach and coach: The set-up is meant to improve the protégé and that is why you should consciously listen to them to understand their needs from their perspective

before you offer a solution. Efforts as leaders/mentors to delegate responsibilities and allow team members or protégés to grow must be accompanied by encouragement, insights, and reflective questions. We only provide as much support as is needed and step in when there is no other choice after laying the right path. Always give emotional support, validation and compliments.

5. Create other support networks or referral links: Find ways for your protégé or team members to see other leadership models and approaches. It may be that we recommend them to serve on committees and task forces elsewhere in the organization and region. It might be an encouragement to take a course or attend seminars to see other perspectives and find their style. Regardless, the point is that we need to support exposure to multiple models or mentors.

6. Avoid imposing limitations: We need to shelve our egos and allow others to shine and take pride in what they can accomplish. Some will even surprise us once they begin to develop, and in some areas, they will be better than we are. You can share dreams and goals but encourage them to step outside the box, explore and do more.

Other important qualities a mentor must possess and must be easily transferred during a nurturing exercise include:

Trust

Patience

Responsibility

Empathy

Self-Reliance

Resilience

Adaptability etc.

IMPORTANCE OF NURTURING

A successful mentorship relationship depends on establishing and nurturing a friendly, encouraging and supportive mentor-mentee developmental interaction. Some young professionals or entrepreneurs would love to take credit for creating something on their own. However, the reality is that, while you may have a great idea, you may not know exactly what you should be doing with your business and at which time to develop it into a sustainable business.

Mentors help you begin a successful business, academic, entrepreneurial or any professional career by providing information and knowledge: Mentorship begins at birth and continues throughout life. Parents are the first mentors. A life-giving leadership will naturally encourage movement through the various stages. With the right mentor from the start, the protégé taps into a wealth of knowledge that will get him/her up faster and shorten the learning curve.

Mentors offer the right diagnosis and point you to areas of your personal lives or career that need improvement: Once you sign up with the right mentor because they have passed through your current state successfully, it becomes effortless for them to identify what your faults are and proffer appropriate solutions. This constructive criticism will help put you on the right path. Think of a new driver who struggles to reverse his car and keeps making a particular mistake; but once a professional arrives, he makes necessary corrections by pointing the learner to the things he has not been doing well.

Mentors stimulate personal and professional growth in their protégés: Recall the story of Samuel who at a time was only used to hearing and receiving instructions from Eli. There came a time in his career when God had a direct message for Eli's mentee. No matter the number of times he heard God's voice, he couldn't decipher where it was coming from until Eli, who is used to hearing directly from God, taught him how to respond. Mentors set various goals for you and watch to see how achieving them would help you grow and develop new leadership abilities on your own.

Good mentors never let you quit, their encouragement keeps you going: According to Oprah Winfrey, "A mentor is someone who allows you to see the hope inside yourself". We all could quit easily if not for the hope we receive from those around us. My father tells me stories of the times in his life when he could have quitted but found the strength to go on. Stories like this, of breakthroughs during a breaking point, help mentees to push on. Mothers tell their daughters where they find the strength to remain in marriages and this saves them from divorce. On several occasions, Dr Ben Carson would have given up, but his mother kept encouraging him. He now looks back to those moments and uses them to encourage others.

Mentors instil discipline and help create boundaries: There are many important dos and don'ts in life with overwhelming consequences but parents and other mentors help us create boundaries early enough. Proverbs 22:6 – "Train a child in the way he should go, and when he is old he will not depart from it". Without the proper care of a farmer, some crops will be stunted or grow wild because of the overbearing influence of many contending factors. In trying to achieve one's goals, friends, family, peers, other unserious colleagues or even oneself, may try to pull you off course. The benefits of discipline include solid work ethics, sharpened focus, clarified priorities, and attainment of goals, among others. Recall Moses's mother drawing his ear and telling him not to forget he's a Hebrew and not an Egyptian, a lesson he never forgot until his death.

Mentors are priceless: We pay heavily to learn basic knowledge in schools but real-life school is free. A mentorship relationship will grow organically through connections within your industry and network. Can you pay your father for being your father? Or your mentor? Their time, knowledge, skills, and experiences as well as their networks come to us for free most times. They are driven by the satisfaction of your success and that the knowledge, through you, will empower others. If I am asked to pay back all I've benefitted from all my mentors, I would perpetually be in debt. But I have resolved to pay it forward, and this book is one way I intend to do that.

CHAPTER FOUR

TRANSFORMED

The major goal of mentorship is to transform the mentee so he/she may be able to achieve their set goals, as well as develop the capacity to help others like him/her. Mentors help you determine whom you want to become, how you must change to become such a person, and how you can take advantage of their experiences and those of others to bring about these changes. Mentoring takes different forms and stages, although the process is not cast in stone. The length of time for the change to become visible may be individual-specific. In some cases, it may be a lifetime course, others may be intermittent and as the need arises, while some may be a short or immediate encounter, with both the work and impact felt. Other people may categorize mentorship into a formal arrangement such as between a student and an adviser in undergraduate or graduate schools, or informal relationships that people develop throughout their careers. 17

At one time or another, we all realize that trying to do great things is difficult. Trying to do them alone is, more often than not, impossible. That is why all great leaders have mentors, and they also mentor others. No matter how competitive you feel about your skills – especially during the early stage of your career – success is, in reality, a team sport. When you are coached by the best, and you play according to the rules, you become the best, and as expected, you make others better too.

A good mentor is a transformational leader. A transformational leader enhances the motivation, morale and performance of followers in a variety of ways. These may include; connecting the follower's sense of identity to his mission and the collective identity of the organization or career group; being a role model that inspires their followers; challenging followers to take greater ownership of their work; understanding the strength and weaknesses of followers; be able to align them with tasks that optimize their performance. The mentor achieves the transformation of his protégés through:

Articulation of a vision that is inspiring and appealing to his mentees.

Challenging them with high standards, communicating optimism and providing meaning and a sense of purpose.

Supporting the mentees' development through strong communication skills, and conveying messages compellingly and persuasively.

Challenging assumptions with quality and relevant experiences, taking risks and soliciting the mentees' ideas on critical issues.

Displaying conviction, taking a stand and appealing to mentees on an emotional level with a clear set of values.

Stimulating and encouraging creativity.

Providing appropriate platforms for the mentees to accomplish their goals.

Educating and propelling them to further achievement and growth.

Mentorship is a psychosocial function according to Kathy Kram.18 It enables leaders to motivate others to do more than they originally intended or thought possible. The mentor works with his protégé to set challenging expectations to achieve higher performance and this exercise requires commitment on both sides. It pays attention to individual needs and personal development and helps mentees develop their leadership skills. Research has shown that mentoring is about change, transition and leadership. When the work is done appropriately, the product, like light, cannot be hidden.

EXAMPLES OF GREAT LEADERS THAT WERE TRANSFORMED AFTER BEING MENTORED

1. Moses

Moses, like any other mentee, had continued his work in his own little but inexperienced way, making a lot of mistakes;

sometimes offending God, and this affected those he led negatively. Moses had to grapple with leading about four hundred thousand (400,000) footmen. This number neither includes the women nor children that left Egypt for Canaan on foot. Consider the distance they were to cover and the overwhelming challenges they faced on the way; now, imagine the enormous responsibility of leading such a multitude. The story of Moses shows what young people, business and career beginners go through without the care, guidance or encouragement of a mentor.

His story changed when he came into a mentorship with Jethro, the Priest of Midian, who later became his father-in-law. Moses had a special relationship with him. Though he had been raised with all the wisdom and education in Egypt, he learned more about leadership from the priest and shepherd, Jethro, whose flocks Moses tended until his call at Sinai. Jethro visited Moses and observed as he settled disputes among the children of Israel. The Lord made Moses fit to settle disputes among the children of Israel but taking up all the responsibilities by himself was a burden, hence, Jethro's advice to delegate the job of settling disputes.

The lessons learned from Moses's mentorship exposure include:

It is important to bring in or allow other voices of wisdom.

It is good to hear hard words, no matter how difficult it seems at the beginning.

It is important to comply with the advice you received no matter where it comes from.

Don't die in silence, share your burdens with the right people – they will help make it light.

It is good to recognize leadership capacity. He made leaders of 10s, leaders of 50s, leaders of 100s and leaders of 1000s. When you see yourself as only worthy of some duties, it limits you and the job suffers.

It is good to get involved and stay involved. After the division of labour, Moses never had to judge the Israelites all by himself again. In the same way, all the challenges of judging alone never resurfaced.

It is important to apply the wise advice you are given. If not, the problem will persist until you can effect the change.

Mentors are invaluable, they help you engage impossibilities and convert them to skills.

Other ways mentorship can change your life for the better:

You will never have to face hardships or challenges alone. With a good mentor on your speed dial, always willing to give you an attentive ear, you can easily overcome those helpless feelings of isolation.

A mentor will help you discover the keys to unlocking your natural talents and how best to use them to influence the world around you.

Mentors answer your deep questions in transformative ways that put you in the right direction, both in life and career.

Sometimes we need a superhero to cheer us on and nudge us forward through the darkness. Someone to remind us that, come what may, we always have an ally and a choice. They are like cheerleaders, who relentlessly boost your self-esteem and confidence until you feel brave enough to step over your boundaries.

With good mentors, nothing is off-limits. We find the courage to share private thoughts and concerns and are certain to get the right counsel.

Mentors are challengers who question your comfort zone until it no longer exists. They insist you have not done enough if it is not your best.

Selecting a mentor can be one of life's most important decisions. Mentors are crucial when people get to a phase that requires the development of new knowledge, skills or attitude. When you get this right, the transition becomes seamless. Like an expert travel companion, a mentor will help you navigate your way in the right direction. After all, they have been through similar routes, perhaps made mistakes, and know the pitfalls to avoid. This was true in the life and leadership of Moses.

2. Steve Jobs mentoring Mark Zuckerberg:

When Facebook's founder struggled during his early days, he turned to one of his mentors, Steve Jobs for advice. Jobs had one tip for him: 'Pack your bags for India'. According to Mark, "Early on in our history when things weren't going well – we had hit a rough patch and a lot of people wanted to buy Facebook. I met with Steve Jobs, and he said that to reconnect with what I believed was the mission of this company, I should visit this temple in India that he had gone to early in the evolution of Apple when he wanted his vision of the future to be". And that small piece of advice, to cultivate your mentor relationship, is the most applicable takeaway from Zuckerberg's travel tale.19

Zuckerberg visited the temple and travelled around India for a month. He saw how people in India connected and it affirmed his sense of Facebook's mission. "That reinforced to me the importance of what we were doing, and that is something I will always remember" – Zuckerberg. These two legends are renowned for their revolutionary impact on global IT and social networking. They were said to have taken walks around Palo Alto, discussing how Zuckerberg might manage and develop Facebook, as well as entrepreneurship. In 2011, upon Steve's death, Mark Zuckerberg posted "Steve, thank you for being a mentor and a friend. Thanks for showing that what you build can change the world. I will miss you." The success story of Facebook and many other endeavours of Mark will not be complete without mentioning the transformational impact of his mentor, Steve Jobs.

3. Maya Angelou mentoring Oprah Winfrey:

Yes, it's true – even Oprah had a mentor! Oprah Winfrey's friendship with Maya Angelou began in her 20s when Oprah was a reporter and had the opportunity to interview the poet. At this time, Oprah had already felt the power in Angelou's poem "I Know Why the Caged Bird Sings", which she claimed validated her personal experience. As years goes by, these two American icons became close friends. Angelou went on to become what Oprah described as a "mentor-mother-sister-friend". She gave several pieces of advice that changed her approach to life and career.20

Oprah continued by saying, 'She was there for me always, guiding me through some of the most important years of my life. Mentors are important, and I don't think anybody makes it in this world without some form of mentorship.' Many people today look up to Oprah Winfrey for her iconic mastery in her field as a TV host, and the world pays her for it. This feat didn't come by her efforts alone, Maya Angelou played a significant role alongside.

4. Warren Buffett mentoring Bill Gates:

These are two of the world's most successful businessmen and philanthropists, Bill Gates and his close friend, the CEO of Berkshire Hathaway, Warren Buffet. Bill Gates claimed that Warren Buffet changed his life by teaching him about the true measure of success. According to Buffet, it is not by your net worth but by having the people you care about love you in return. He admits that over the years, he has turned to Buffett for advice on various subjects and has referred to him as one-of-a-kind. The billionaires' relationship greatly affected their life and businesses, and the world bears witness to how they revolutionized their respective business sectors and gave back to society through charities. Who would have thought that Bill Gates needed a mentor? He, in turn, now mentors thousands of businessmen and women.

5. Mahatma Gandhi mentoring Nelson Mandela:

Many know Mahatma Gandhi as a Nobel Peace Prize winner but only a few knew him as a great mentor. Under Gandhi's mentorship, Martin Luther King Jnr. and Nelson Mandela flourished and made great impacts that inspired millions of people in their time. Although they never met, Mandela was greatly influenced by the writings and life of Gandhi. The lessons he learnt enabled him to take heroic steps in ending apartheid in South Africa and he became one of the greatest leaders Africa ever produced.

6. Sir Freddie Laker mentoring Richard Branson

Mentorship is a vital component of success, which is why mentors focus on giving their students guidance, not only in academics but in all walks of life. Richard Branson while commenting on his earliest mentor, said, "If you ask any successful business person, they must have had a great mentor at some point along the road. It's always good to have a helping hand at the start. I wouldn't have gotten anywhere in the airline industry without the mentorship of Sir Freddie Laker. Now, I love mentoring young entrepreneurs". Branson went to Laker during his struggles to get Virgin Atlantic up and running. Now as one of the most successful businessmen of all time, he doesn't think he could have made it without the help of Freddie Laker. As a result of Laker's advice and guidance, Branson was able to grow his business and understand the risks worth taking.21

7. Michael Jordan mentoring Kobe Bryant

As a child, Kobe Bryant was obsessed with Michael Jordan, and he studied him to learn how to compete with big players. He emulated Jordan's mannerisms and techniques so closely that by the time he arrived at the NBA, he could replicate Jordan's moves completely. When they finally met, they developed a mentor-mentee relationship which had a huge impact on Bryant's career. Jordan took Bryant under his wing and advised him on the practice required and lifestyle choices needed to succeed in the NBA. Bryant said, "I don't think people understand the amount of impact he's had on me as a player and as a leader".22

The lists above are powerful examples of great leaders, captains of industries and those who helped them in great measures to become successful. However, there are countless numbers of unpublished men and women who are being transformed daily, who may not be as rich as Bill Gates but are getting help to become better. As a mentor, you will be making someone's dreams come through faster, and soon enough, we will be able to tell their stories too. So, keep up the good work.

To someone with big dreams; there is help for you out there. Get a mentor to become transformed from your current level, and get closer to achieving your dreams. At the end of this book, we have put together some great minds so that you won't have to look too far.

CHAPTER FIVE

OPTIMISTIC

Just as it is important to check automobiles for problems from time to time, it is equally important, if not more, to check what drives people to give their best and what makes them willing to do more until they are confident they have given their best. Optimism embraces the concepts of inclination towards hope and the tendency to believe that we will have the best outcomes in life. Over the years, there has been significant research about the effectiveness of optimism as a psychological phenomenon, leading to different postulations. One of the findings is that optimism is an emotional competence that can help boost productivity, enhance employee morale, overcome conflicts and have an overall positive impact.

It is expected that everyone should have elements of optimism. Everyone at one time or another has dreams and expectations for their future, but not all continue to expect the same as time goes on. Some believe that someday, they will rise to become inventors, entrepreneurs, doctors, surgeons, pilots, police officers, philosophers, etc. There may be people encouraging us to stay on course, reminding us often of our dreams and doing all they can to ensure our dreams come through. Sadly, there are also detractors, who for one reason or another, are either uninterested in your dreams, make you believe your dreams are impossible, or actively work against your progress. The optimist views life from a different perspective and generally come up with positive and successful outcomes in all situations. Mentors are very helpful in making people view life from a more optimistic perspective.

Mentors and other transformational leaders have high degrees of optimism themselves, which help them generate the energy and commitment necessary to achieve results. They do well to inspire the same amount of optimism in their mentees and followers at all levels. Conversely, pessimists have a negative influence on themselves and others, and these impact an organization's creativity and innovation. To be innovative, you should be open to new ideas, see possibilities, willing to take risks and encourage others to do the same, and be willing to challenge the status quo to create new solutions, products or improve processes. Summarily, you need to be adventurous and expect success. Those with a pessimistic outlook on life typically approach changes to the status quo with familiar words such as; "We have tried this before", "It won't work", or "It will never fly". Such individuals often label themselves as 'devil's advocate'. How can someone who has a pessimistic outlook embrace change over the safety of the known?

Optimism has been shown to have a direct or indirect effect on an individual's health, academics, finances, career, job satisfaction and general outlook on life. This is equally true about pessimism. Dr Martin E. P. Seligman,[23] the modern scholar most often associated with studying the traits of optimists, and former president of the American Psychological Association and Professor of Psychology at the University of Pennsylvania, devoted decades to studying optimistic people and reported three traits that are common in all. They view adversity as temporary, specific and external, that is, it is not entirely their fault; as opposed to pessimists who view adversity as unchangeable, pervasive, and more personal. In the face of setbacks, challenges or difficult jobs, pessimists are more likely to perform worse than predicted and even give up, while optimists will persevere. Optimism, therefore, is also an important component of achievement and is especially important in times of chaos, change and turbulence. Those who have an optimistic outlook will roll with the punches, be more proactive and persistent, and will not abandon hope.

Mentorship can leave a person feeling good about themselves. When a person does something good such as mentoring and helping others, they feel positive, knowing that they have the chance to make a difference. A mentor helps the mentees believe in themselves and build confidence. Their positive approach towards different situations helps them to understand better and be positive. No matter what the situation is, mentors always encourage mentees to do their best and believe that the outcome will be good, just the way an optimist would. Mentors and optimists have a few things in common; they have a positive and progressive way of thinking, they find opportunities in difficult situations, and they inspire others to do positive things. An optimist foresees and expects the best to happen. "The pessimist sees difficulty in every opportunity. The optimist sees the opportunity in every difficulty"24

HELPFUL STRATEGIES TO BECOME AN OPTIMIST

Avoid toxic environments: This may be difficult to achieve sometimes. Make effort to seek the company of positive individuals around you and in your organization. This may mean fraternizing with peers of like minds in other departments. Endeavour to stay away from professional complainers. Successful people choose or create the kind of companies they keep. Mentors and parents alike, help sift the kind of people or environment we grow in. As the popular saying goes; 'show me your friend and I can tell who you are'.

Focus on and celebrate your strengths: The key to great achievement and happiness is to play out your strengths, not correct your weaknesses. You need to focus on what you do well. Good mentors come in handy here. As earlier said, mentors enable their protégés to identify their areas of strength and continue to help them improve on them. For example, due to the poor education system in Nigeria, most students want to major in sciences, maybe due to the popularity of such fields. But with the right guidance, you may find out that these students would do better in arts or other vocational areas.

Nurture a culture of optimism around you: Doing this makes optimism become a part of you and those around you. Expect people to succeed. They may occasionally fail to achieve what they set out to do, encourage them regardless so that they can tackle the challenge another time. Teach children that they may fail sometimes, but that real failure comes when you stop trying. That way, the home will reek of positivity, and they will grow with it, and teach others the same.

Take care of your spiritual and emotional well-being: By reading the Bible and other inspirational materials daily, you will grow a healthy mindset and develop a positive outlook on life. This may be different for each person. Some may be inspired by daily quotations; others by reading about innovations around the world, especially those relevant to their chosen career path. Different religious groups have many great resources in this regard.

Embrace freshness in nature: When working on a difficult task, fatigue or boredom might set in, and without a positive response, it will look like you are incapacitated. Take some time out and visit the beach, a waterfall or other recreational sites. Outdoor life is a positive life; you enjoy fresh air, gaze at beautiful plantations and most importantly, see people who are less skilled or privileged embracing positivity.

Manage the things you cannot change well: Whenever you are faced with setbacks, identify what you can change and proactively do something about it. According to Benjamin Franklin, "While we may not be able to control all that happens to us, we can control what happens inside of us". You can ask for help from someone with the skill you lack, seek a mentor, or collaborate with others.

Cultivate spontaneity: Consider putting aside your plans once in a while to take a walk with your kids, play a game or watch a show. Getting out of your comfort zone by being spontaneous help to develop an optimistic mind, as spontaneity involves an expectation of a pleasurable experience. Doing spontaneous things increases your skill set and this, in turn, boosts optimism.

Consider the health importance: Evidence suggests that the immune systems of optimists are stronger than that of pessimists. Have you noticed that the more you are afraid of a certain outcome, the more they tend to occur? If you need extra motivation to practice optimism, consider the statistics linking optimism to good health.

EXAMPLES OF OPTIMISM BOOSTERS

Many may not appreciate the importance of lifting another's morale in the face of difficulties until they have the need and there will be no one to come to their aid. Sportsmen and women from time to time, especially during the early stage of their career, struggle with failure and often fear relegation; but a good coach will always do his best to boost their courage by helping them remain optimistic. A baker, fashion designer, young entrepreneur, or even a young faculty member, as in other fields of endeavour, has low moments and needs someone at one point or another to convince them about why they should go on.

1. Paul and Timothy: The mentorship relationship between Apostle Paul and his protégé, Timothy, shows mentors truly inspire optimism in their mentees; the same goes for other great and transformational leaders. In 2 Timothy chapters 1 & 2, Paul instructs Timothy not to cower in the sight of challenges or oppositions that are imminent. "For God has not given us the spirit of fear, but of power and love and sound mind." – 2 Timothy 1:7. This method was consistent with Paul and his protégés, and it proved successful every time.

2. Frank McCotter and Ben Carson: Mr McCotter was Ben's high school biology teacher and is regarded as the second mentor in his life. According to Ben Carson, "Mr McCotter treated me as though my opinions counted; he also knew how to stimulate my interest without making me feel pushed or manipulated. For him, no doubts existed about my abilities to do any outstanding project; he simply wanted to offer guidance. Mr McCotter did much for my sense of self-esteem: because he believed in my ability, I was able to believe in it as well."[25]

3. Steve Jobs and Mark Zuckerberg: This is a story we all can relate to, especially because of the success of the protégé

and how this influences up-comers. Recall in the previous chapter that early in his career, Mark got several offers to sell his company but when he encountered his mentor, Steve Jobs helped him find the meaning of his mission. After the trip to India and his observation about the power of social interactions, he recounted; "That reinforced to me the importance of what we were doing, and that is something I will always remember".

4. Mordecai and Esther: This story encourages me anytime I read it. Unknown to Esther, her leadership ability was been developed, but similar to everyone else, life presents difficult moments that lead to advancement. Her mentor, Mordecai believed in her ability to change the terrible situation her people found themselves in at the time. On her own, she feared the situation would consume her. To boost her courage, Mordecai remarked, "If you remain completely silent at this time, relief and deliverance will arise for the Jews from another place... yet who knows whether you have come to the kingdom for such a time as this?" – Esther 4:14.

What Do You See?

Nurturing positive thoughts and emotions about your situations impacts one's well-being and indirectly, others around you. It is important to note that our lives are not lived in a vacuum, we must live in a way that benefits others. Many people around you have or are losing confidence in themselves and no longer believe a change is possible. A well-articulated social support and connectedness will, to a large extent, influence their emotional, physical, spiritual and mental health.

A story is told of two patients in a hospital ward. One was placed near the window and the other, a little far from the window. Each day, the man beside the window would encourage his partner with news of how beautiful and sunny the day was, and how he wish to leave soon to go and enjoy the fresh air outside and admire the beautiful vegetation. The second patient, however, was always melancholic and cried about how life has dealt with him badly. The man by the window got better and was discharged while the second patient requested to be moved to the particular spot where his neighbour stayed so that he will also enjoy the view. The nurses then inform him that the other patient was a blind man and couldn't have seen anything at all.

The positive effects of hope and optimism impact human life at all stages, races and vocations. There are times we may feel trapped by events and circumstances that befall us; such as the patient in the story above. You are not alone! Choose to be optimistic, and take advantage of the numerous supports around you, especially the inspiring promises in the scriptures. With such assurances, we may celebrate life and enjoy wholeness, even in our brokenness.

INSPIRING QUOTES ON OPTIMISM

"Hope is the twin of optimism" –Florence Ofovwe.

"You don't need to see the whole staircase, just take the first step." — Martin Luther King, Jr.

"What you thought before has led to every choice you have made, and this adds up to you at this moment. If you want to change who you are physically, mentally, and spiritually, you will have to change what you think." – Dr Patrick Gentempo

"The secret of health for both mind and body is not to mourn for the past, not to worry about the future, but to live the present moment wisely and earnestly." – Buddha

"Don't be afraid to give up the good to go for the great." – John D. Rockefeller

"Life is not about finding yourself. Life is about creating yourself." – Lolly Daskal

"There is no passion to be found playing small – in settling for a life that is less than the one you are capable of living." — Nelson Mandela

"You can do what you have to do, and sometimes you can do it even better than you think you can." — Jimmy Carter

"Courage doesn't mean you don't get afraid. Courage means you don't let fear stop you." — Bethany Hamilton

"In any moment of decision, the best thing you can do is the right thing. The worst thing you can do is nothing." – Theodore Roosevelt

"No one is perfect, that's why pencils have erasers." — Wolfgang Riebe

"Be the change you wish to see in the world." — Mahatma Gandhi

"If my mind can conceive it, and my heart can believe it, then I can achieve it." — Muhammad Ali

"You are not here merely to make a living. You are here to enable the world to live more amply, with greater vision, and with a finer spirit of hope and achievement. You are here to enrich the world, and you impoverish yourself if you forget the errand." — Woodrow Wilson

"You can do no more than you believe you can. You can be no more than you believe you are." — Norman Vincent Peale

Here is my acronym of the word OPTIMISTIC:

O   OFTEN

P   POSITIVE

T   THROUGH

I	INCONGRUOUS
M	MOMENTS, but
I	INITIATING
S	STRATEGIES
T	TAILORED towards
I	IMPROVING
C	COURAGEOUSLY

The Optimistic are those who are Often Positive Through Incongruous Moment, but keep on Initiating Strategies, Tailored towards Improving their situations Courageously.

CHAPTER SIX

REASSURED

Gift was a new sales representative in a Multi-National Insurance Company, who was starting her career at a time when the insurance market was not at its peak. First, she struggled to develop a passion for the job as she tries to close new policy accounts. Gift was fortunate to have her line manager/unit head, Mrs Odia, who had put in about 20 years to this career and has major policy accounts to her credit. Like many sales jobs, Gift's earnings were dependent on the commission from her policy accounts, but since she does not have much of that yet, work was not fun at all. As expected of a good mentor and team leader, Mrs Odia made sure Gift learned the techniques of the job; took her out for marketing drives and exposed her to new clients and emerging ways of closing policy accounts. She also called daily to make sure the new skills are being applied. She ensured that Gift followed up with her prospects, and from time to time, monitored her well-being.

According to Pablo Picasso, "Every child is an artist. The problem is how to remain an artist once he grows up". After her maternity leave, Gift desired a new job that would pay her salary at the end of the month so she could support her family, rather than relying on commission from her scarce policy accounts. When she resumed duty, the weekly review meetings aimed at encouraging the sales representatives, appraising their performance, and consolidating new strategies, became rather unattractive to Gift because of her low productivity. But encouragement from her husband and reassurances from Mrs Odia awakened new zeal and a growing passion for building a career in sales. In her words, "I have the best mentors around me and the impact of their relationship, with God's grace, is the reason for my success, I am no more dulling".

Reassurance can be defined as a special kind of education that counteracts fear. Reassurance relieves or removes unnecessary anxiety, especially regarding one's physical or emotional health. It is the physician's most commonly used type of counselling. Reassurance is very therapeutic. Parents need some reassurance during almost every office visit or phone call. Reassurance is more likely to be effective if certain guidelines are followed.26 According to Oxford University Press, reassurance is the removal of fears and concerns about an illness.27

As parents, we give our children or wards assurances of a beautiful and secure future. Some have and share big dreams for their children; they call them their special doctors, nurses, pilots, engineers, architects etc., and all these get across to the children as well. Most young people grow up with this wonderful outlook on life; with confidence, believing their parents must walk them through achieving these great aspirations. But unfortunately, the truth is that not all turn out as wonderful. As a traveller, you start your journey with excitement, but fatigue gradually sets in as you go farther, and with the right encouragement, you arrive at your destination safely. We all need reassurance that we are on track, we are capable of finishing strong, and we have the unwavering support of family, friends, colleagues, partners and importantly, our mentors.

Mentors are like tour guides; they check the maps to note how far the journey is and how best to get to the set destination with minimal effort. They point out landmarks and give guidance on the best ways to navigate through them. Mentors remind you of the reason you started the journey in the first place. Recall the story of Mark Zuckerberg and Steve Jobs at a time when the Facebook enterprise suffered a decline during the early stage (to the point that other businesses offered to buy over the company). The tour to India as advised by Steve Jobs helped him reach his inner conviction about their set mission, and reacquaint himself and his partner with why they had set out in the first place. The result of this intervention speaks for itself, to the admiration of everyone.

HOW TO EFFECTIVELY GIVE REASSURANCE TO YOUR MENTEES

Choose the right time: Because of our relationships, we often feel obligated to lift the spirit of our dear ones when we notice they are afraid or down. To do this without tact will only complicate or make matters worse. So, do not be too hasty or too early to reassure someone. Choose the right time. Rather than quickly saying your bit and throttling off, make yourself available to them, make them feel understood, be patient and when the right atmosphere presents itself, use it well and promise to walk them through as much as it's possible. Most sympathizers are often passive, but to effectively reassure, find the best time and make the most of it. Only when your child, mentee, patient or friend believes that you have explored the problem adequately and understood it, will the reassurance be more acceptable.

Be specific and focused: Blanket reassurances like 'everything will be fine', or 'there is nothing to worry about', may cause the person you are trying to assist to feel you are being insensitive or dishonest, and this would have defeated the purpose of reassurance. If the issue is about your child struggling with some subjects, your mentee's business having difficulty in breaking through the market, or a parent afraid of their child developing a brain tumour after recurrent headaches; speak to the specific issue. There is no panacea when it comes to giving reassurances. When the precise overriding fear is identified, the physician or mentor can carefully investigate that specific concern and offer reassurances when the fear is unfounded. You need to demonstrate kind and thoughtful gestures, offer physical touch if appropriate and remind them of the positive traits that have helped them in the past.

Be an active listener: Active listening is an attempt to truly understand the content and emotion of what the other person is saying, by paying attention to verbal and non-verbal messages. The task is to focus, hear, respect, and communicate your desire to understand. This is not the time to be planning a response or conveying how you feel.28 Mentors and parents care about their mentees or children's progress in school, career plan, and personal development. So, when they raise any concern in an important area, you need to pay active attention and allow them to lead the conversation. No matter how similar your experiences are, allow your mentees to express themselves freely and you must appear to genuinely care. Maintain eye contact and give them full attention. Many people think that being a mentor requires special skills, but mentors are simply people who have the qualities of good role models.

Be honest: Have your parents told you how they were always the best in their class all through their school days; especially when they are trying to get you to work on your grades? Whatever you tell your child, protégé or anyone in need of reassurance must be honest. This is because, when you are caught in one lie, the remainder of your assurances are questionable. Imagine how you would feel if you find out someone has lied to you in matters you hold dear. You don't need to reveal everything on your mind; the truth might be that the situation cannot be salvaged immediately. Any nonessential information that may produce anxiety should be withheld rather than misleading them.

Give reassurance with facts: Your interest in reassuring someone is not enough and of course, the entire exercise depends largely on who and what needs to be addressed. When you pay close attention to your child, mentee or junior colleague, you will be able to direct your interventions appropriately. For each of the issues raised, give the best and verifiable advice or compare similar cases with a known solution. Make referrals where necessary.

Keep it brief: For your reassurance to be effective, it must be in a few words. Most people just want to hear, in a few words, the possible outcome of their situation. When you prolong your speech, you provoke the fear that perhaps you are hiding your true feeling and worries behind your long speech. Let them know that they won't always feel this way and give support to help them face the fear.

You do not need to speak sometimes: Nonverbal communication often passes the message more than words. As a physician can examine a patient's heart without wearing a worried facial expression, so will your time, solidarity visits, gifts and other important nonverbal gestures give reassuring support. You could offer to take him or her to a movie or favourite sports and root for them. In more ways than verbal rhetoric, show that you care.

Give a universal context: Let them know that they are not alone in whatever they may be facing. You can give comfort by commenting on the universality of the problem when appropriate. Something like, "Do you know that one in every three business start-ups encounter capital-related problems? So you are not alone". This can go a long way to alleviate anxiety. The identified issues may be part of ongoing situations and conditions that mentees face, so mentors need to be trained to support and accept these aspects of the mentees' lives without judgment. Mentors and mentoring programs should not focus heavily on changing behaviour when issues arise, rather, they should seek accurate information and give the best help as much as possible.

Refer: You do not need to have a lasting solution to all issues. In areas where you are not so skilled, you need to refer your mentees. There may be issues of grave concern that generally require direct and immediate intervention. Some of these issues, like child abuse and neglect, are mandated by law to be reported to the appropriate authorities; others may require a referral to a known institution for direct intervention. In addition, many of these issues require collaboration with the families of mentees, and this should be handled by mentors with specialized skill sets.

From the list above, one of the benefits of mentorship is that the mentee has someone to rely on when the going gets tough. When you try to live your life in isolation, you expose your life, dreams or passion to sudden death in the face of overwhelming challenges and just like a lone walker; no one can come to your rescue. So, get connected with a mentor, family, religious group, or professional network to refill you whenever you are running dry. Be reassured!

OTHER BENEFITS OF REASSURANCE

Enables you to connect to your first fire (passion).

Boosts your confidence.

Keeps you on course.

Improves and sharpens your skills.

Connects you to a valuable and resourceful network.

Reminds you that you are not alone.

Equips you to encourage others.

CHAPTER SEVEN

ENTRUSTED

"One important key to success is self-confidence. An important key to self-confidence is preparation." - Arthur Ashe

Every tree that is planted, watered, nurtured and well-pruned, matures to bear fruits. In the same way, mentees are expected to bear fruits while chasing their dreams. Every child well nurtured either by parents or other important caregivers will someday grow up to take over the family's estate. Mentees are like apprentices, who after successful completion of their training schedules, are released to establish their businesses and to prosper in them. Sometimes, they take over the business space of their masters or major in specialized areas to create a niche for themselves.

The idea of training in business environments and organizations is for new employees to take over the management of the organizations in the future. Mentors equip their protégés with the requisite knowledge and deploy them to solve problems in specialized areas of society or assign them roles to test their readiness. These assignments are closely monitored to identify areas of deficit, which are corrected appropriately. Organizations that do not train their workforce for leadership will not grow, and this will make them less competitive in the market. At one time or another, the role of leadership or management may fall on employees who were once new, whether they were adequately prepared or not.

It is said that practice makes perfect. You must allow your child or mentee to implement the lessons they have acquired in real-life situations. Entrusting them with important roles will straighten their hands until they become perfect. And of course, you delegate such duties to those who show strong indications of readiness to engage in the real world. To entrust anything to anyone, you must believe they are capable to handle such. Trust is an important aspect of mentorship, as well as any other training program. It requires you to be able to identify those with special skills, readiness and humility. Trust must be earned, and it takes time. An athlete needs training and more training before the coach will nominate them for important tournaments. So, during a tournament, the coach or the team management fields only athletes that they trust to bring the prize home. The amount of dedication and thoroughness put into preparation by both the athlete and coaching crew will determine the result in the end.

The timing for such releases or delegations must be accurate. If the athlete or mentee is released too early, they may not have acquired sufficient skills and stamina to withstand adverse conditions, nor be able to survive the competition or harsh business environment. When you release them too late, they become dependent and may find it difficult to ever be ready for anything. Good mentorship can be likened to an irrigation system that allows information and knowledge to flow to where it is needed, at a rate and in a manner that can be absorbed easily.

FEEDBACK

Learning is simply the process of soliciting, receiving, and integrating feedback. If the mentee is to learn from the mentor and vice versa, they must be giving and receiving regular feedback. Giving and receiving feedback focused on improvement and goal accomplishment is a skill. The greater the amount of accurate, skillfully delivered feedback in a mentorship relationship, the better the quality of that relationship and the lessons derived. Both mentors and mentees need training in the giving and receiving of feedback. It has to be the measure of accountability for their entire relationship. Developing and honing those feedback skills need to remain 'front and centre' throughout the course of the mentor/mentee relationship. When this is rightly done, the leader or mentor will be confident that he has successfully tutored his mentee and will be bold to encourage independence, while the mentee is satisfied to have received the best training to engage in any task.

Giving and receiving feedback is not just one of the key skills for learning from a mentor/mentee, it is a major leadership and management skill developed by the mentor/mentee relationship. Mentor/mentee partners grow in their ability to share feedback, information and knowledge. These are the exact abilities required for organizations to grow in their capacity to learn, change and navigate an ever-complex world.

THE PROCESS OF LEGACY LEADERSHIP

Mentorship is perhaps one of the most powerful methods by which we can shape the future. The highest point of leadership/mentorship is reached when a leader/mentor teaches his or her followers to live successfully without depending on them. Leaders at this level teach others how to lead themselves. As noted earlier, this does not happen immediately; it is a gradual but intentional process that requires skill and time. The following model will help us develop legacy leaders/mentees:

Show the Right Example:

A central aspect of mentorship is the act of teaching. Mentors teach their protégés, first and foremost. Parents, leaders, and mentors prepare their protégés to develop a better version of themselves but they do this with their knowledge and experiences. Leaders lay concrete footpaths for others to follow. A mentor must be well-behaved at all times, both publicly and privately, as if their protégé is their shadow. Part of the mentorship process is the act of demonstration as the protégé 'shadows' the mentor, the proper methods, techniques, practices, and procedures that are part of the way the enterprise functions. Beyond this, is the need for the mentor to show the protégé how a professional deal with various challenges and opportunities. A mentor should be a model of composure, dignity, integrity, and professionalism, under all circumstances. A protégé who shadows such a role model will eventually come to understand, at a deeper level, what he or she must be and do. A successful protégé is willing to listen, observe, learn, and grow from the example of another.

Do It with Me:

Children love to mimic their parents, and that's how they learn. One of the best ways to transfer knowledge or new skills is for both the teacher and student to do the exercise. Lessons of this type do not lend themselves to a quick one-time demonstration. This is not an easy, by-the-numbers, single-shot process. A person becomes a mentor and a role model through persistent effort and interaction with the protégé over a considerable period. A mentor can teach the basics of a task at hand fairly quickly, but what distinguishes mentorship from simply teaching or training is that it requires prolonged involvement. You cannot model optimal actions over a broad spectrum of conditions at once or at will; it must happen naturally, in its own time. An effective mentor is like an elephant that tramples down high grass and flattens bushes to ease the way for the younger, quicker animals. People differ in the way they learn. For people who learn by reading, the mentor must provide a written set of resources to the protégé, complete with instructions on where to look for further help. Some learn by watching others perform the task in question (e.g., apprentices), so the mentor must model the appropriate behaviour. This method is mostly adopted by parents, and in many regards, this boosts the confidence of the children. When parents are no longer there, the children will leverage their firsthand experiences.

You Do It, Let Me Watch:

Encourage those under your mentorship to fail as often as necessary to learn the craft you want them to learn. When a mentor puts his/herself in the protégé's stiff, squeaky new shoes, he or she knows without being told which areas are likely to be causing discomfort and difficulties. The mentor can anticipate problems and needs, and proactively take steps to smooth the path. The protégé will appreciate this because it reduces their countless questions. It shows consideration for the protégé's need for self-respect. Empathy helps form a bond between a mentor and a protégé, thereby fostering the kind of mutual commitment that characterizes mentorship at its best. Recall the story of Moses and Jethro, after training him in the art of taking care of sheep, observed the great challenges he faced in leading and judging over 400 thousand men of Israel; Jethro made strong recommendations for division of labour as the only way out of Moses' leadership quagmire. When applied, Moses was better for it. To nurture any human, similar natural laws must be obeyed. We cannot reasonably expect a harvest of expert-level performance from someone who has not had the appropriate training or the time to apply and internalize those training through trial and error. Not only is it unrealistic, but also extremely frustrating to the person who is placed in such an unfair situation. Similarly, it is not enough to give a trainee a computer, or any other tool, if we fail to provide the necessary instructions on how to use it.

Get Used to Doing It Right:

Harvesting is a natural process that abides by certain unchanging principles in a definite sequence. No farmer can reap before sowing nor expect a rich harvest without a sizable prior investment of time, talent, and labour. These seem to be obvious points, but they are often missed by people who are "too busy" to do more than go through the motions of mentorship. There is a difference between nurturing someone and being a mother hen. Good parents must let their children make some decisions on their own, including the inevitable mistakes, and learn to deal with the consequences. Through grappling with difficulties, gradually increasing the degree of autonomy, and living with the aftershocks of bad decisions, children become responsible adults who gain independence from their parents. Same as mentees. So also, good mentors must allow their protégés progressively increase degrees of independence, together with the concomitant responsibility for their actions. The joy of all parents and mentors is to see that their wards are doing well on their own. They allow for independence but continue to give support and expert advice when necessary. Just like Kobe Bryant and Michael Jordan, when the protégé succeeds, the mentor shares the glory, but importantly, the focus from the very start is to make the protégé better.

Get Into a Network:

There should be continuous education. A good mentor introduces the protégé to other people who can also provide support, information, and resources. Networking is vital to effective functioning in the real world, and the mentor should give the protégé a head start on establishing those key contacts. Of course, a mentor cannot simply deliver a network to a protégé as if it were a notebook. Relationships are nontransferable — at least not directly transferable. But it is possible to act as a go-between and a facilitator. The mentor should personally take the protégé to meet as many contacts as possible, one at a time, in their respective work areas. These meetings should rather be informal, under pleasant, icebreaking conditions, to help the protégé establish a relationship with each contact. The protégé can, on his or her own, identify core professional groups they wish to join and share with the mentor, who will assist in making it happen. This means that the bug does not start and end with you, endeavour to refer where and when necessary.

APPLICATION EXERCISE

Elisha and Gehazi with the Shunammite woman: Elisha was a renowned prophet of God who did many miracles that helped reposition the people of God during his days. He mentored Gehazi to perhaps take over from him when he die just as he took over from Elijah. One of the remarkable miracles in their ministry was the gift of a son to a barren woman of Shunem who selflessly brought them into her home and provided for them. When the child died, Elisha entrusted the role of raising him to Gehazi, though with Elisha's staff. This delegation didn't go well even after obeying the instructions and procedure (2 Kings 4:31). However, when Elisha arrived, he sent everyone out, including Gehazi his protégé, and the mother of the dead child.

What do you think went wrong?

What would you do differently? (As Elisha)

What would you do differently? (As Gehazi)

IMPEDIMENTS TO A SUCCESSFUL TRANSFER OF LEGACY/DELEGATION

Sometimes, our children do not follow the paths that we lay for them. They create an entirely new path for themselves, as opposed to our initial plans. This is not to say that they must always comply, but some of such deviations affect them negatively, and every parent would love to avoid them. Mentors too, love to see their protégés follow the legacies and training they have received for their lives and career, but some protégés still fail in real-life situations. As we go through the following points, we will attempt to solve some impediments to a successful delegation/transfer of legacy.

1. Ambiguity

Merely instructing your children, mentees or subordinates to do a task, follow your footsteps, or ask if they can handle it, is unlikely to get the outcome you want. There is a need to ensure that your instructions are sufficiently clear and you are satisfied that they understand. Provide the "what" and the "why" by being explicit with directions and providing context for the assignment. The extra minutes you will spend filling in the details would save you hours of frustration later. Feedback is very important here. It enables your protégés to ask you how you want it done and importantly what the stakes are.

2. Impatience

A sense of urgency can be a real asset when you are running a business. Nevertheless, you have to be mindful of how you communicate it to your staff, mentees or children. Those you train or delegate should be given time to process your instructions and be able to produce the expected result. No one appreciates being rushed unnecessarily. Those who are to become independent should be allowed to grow, develop and eventually mature before the job rests in their hands. For instance, in an official environment, too many texts and emails punctuated with "ASAP" and "top priority" are more likely to produce a shabby piece of work. Patiently wait for the process to be complete, or else, you may have to start all over again.

3. Selfishness

The reason people start a business is to have control over their product, brand, time and life, but mentorship and legacy leadership are entirely different. Making everything about you will affect the outcome of what you do. It can easily become a trap if you insist on managing every tiny detail. Resist the temptation to check in constantly. And, if the work is not done the way you would love, allow for the possibility that it might have been better. Mentorship is about helping your protégés become a better version of themselves and not reproduce you. Parents fall into this trap often, when they choose a career path for their children and wards. For instance, insisting that your child study medicine in school to continue running your hospital business may be counterproductive. They must actively take part in making important life decisions. Mentors should not make arbitrary decisions about what and how protégés should do certain things only because of how others may perceive them (mentors).

4. Too much pressure

Everything should be done with appropriate timing. When you start to teach mathematics, no one starts with algebra. You must allow a step-wise progression, the same with mentorship or legacy leadership. Even when they show signs of quick or faster development, you still have to give age/level-appropriate roles. No commander will send a new cadet to the war front when he/she is not ready. The result will be the same if you give your child or mentee responsibilities they are not ready to handle. Know that when you do, you run the risk of burning them out.

5. Lack of feedback

Mentorship offers continuous education. Some of us who have families of our own, still consult our parents to give insights on particular issues that are not very clear to us. This feedback channel helps to reinforce existing knowledge and opens room to learn new ones. If you give an assignment and find your staff returning frequently with numerous questions punctuated by heavy sighs, resist the urge to withdraw from the task. Smile serenely and say, "What do you think?" Most of the time, they end up answering their questions, and this is a big morale booster.

6. Ingratitude

We tend to glamorize business leaders, but the truth is that every positive contribution is a win for every person in your organization. When someone does a great job, make sure they know it. Your confidence in them is contagious and they will be eager to learn and do more. If you fail to recognize good work or remarkable improvement in your protégés, they will feel unappreciated and low self-esteem may set in.

Mentorship is a partnership, and every stakeholder must learn to acquire the right skill set if it is to be successful. Cultivating awareness about where you fall short and partnering with others who are stronger is very helpful. You will have more time to exercise your creative muscles if you don't insist on doing all the heavy lifting alone.

CHAPTER EIGHT

DETERMINED

It is a common saying that determination is a success. You are the only one to determine how far you are willing to go and when to start or declare yourself unfit for success. All great inventions and achievements begin in the mind. In fact, to a large extent, it ends in the mind too. Your ability to create or envision the future and make plans accordingly is what distinguishes you from passive individuals. Every mentor and mentee rely on each other's determination to achieve any set goals. You are trained to create your future and envision where you desire to be; and if you want it so badly, you stop at nothing until it is achieved. Determination is like a vow you make to yourself that you will succeed; this vow is easier to keep because you know exactly where you are going and when you will arrive. Your self-motivation gets you started and takes you a long way. With encouragement and nurture, your guaranteed success becomes seamless.

Many young and inexperienced people fail to understand the importance of setting proper goals and objectives, or they lack the expertise to make their goals realistic and attainable. Mentors set goals, teach the need for goal setting, and help their protégés master the process of establishing and effectively pursuing these set goals. Determination is the gas that drives the wheels of success.

Most successful people are great at delaying gratification.

Most successful people are great at withstanding temptation.

Most successful people are great at overcoming fear to do what they need to do.

Most successful people set priorities; they do the things they decide are most important.

All successful people failed at different times but they kept getting up until they finally succeeded!

I have learned through my personal experience that while the drive is important, you need to know what you're trading. For example, try to find a balance between your conviction and your connection, so you don't burn bridges or leave a trail of dead bodies in your pursuit of results. Invest in yourself and your relationships during the pursuit of your goals, so that you can enjoy the process. Goals are like a vehicle. They are a means to an end, but not the end themselves. Be careful not to compromise your values along your journey. Good mentorship guarantees you this balance.

BENEFITS OF DETERMINATION

Determination gets you started: It is a popular saying that "if wishes were horses, the lame will ride them". But determination is different; it takes you beyond mere wishes to live the dream. While others stay dreaming and wishing, determination pushes you to start. A journey of a thousand miles, they say, begins with a step. This step can only be taken by the ones determined to succeed. Many wish to live out their dreams and fulfil their purposes but it is difficult to achieve this on their own. I recommend going into a mentorship program if they are determined to succeed. Whatever your desire is, get started, get going, and begin to succeed.

You are transformed by determination: When you get started, it is usually with innate talents which may create opportunities, but you have to put in the work to make those opportunities a reality. Hard work is so important that, even if you have an average level of talent, you can transform what you do have into success through determination. When Jack Ma started, he didn't know how to operate a computer but he wanted to go into the internet business; 16 years down the line, he became the richest man in Asia. With determination, he has grown so much that all countries use his platform.

Determination keeps pushing you forward: Winners never quit and quitters never win. Whether you call it determination, grit, or old-fashioned hard work, the will to keep going is a vital component of success. It is the determination that makes you get better at what you do. Success has different levels. Those with great determination keep getting better in whatever they do; if they achieve ABCD today, they aim for E tomorrow. It is his determination that pushed Usain Bolt to break his Olympic records. He could afford not to come back better and remain average.

Great mentors encourage and expect a determination in their protégés.

Without determination you may lose focus on your goals: This is one of the reasons mentorship is very important, especially for young entrepreneurs and career babes. You may get started with basketball and because your contemporaries are doing better in football, you want to switch. Determination means that as long as you have a goal, you can create paths that lead to that goal, always moving closer to the success you desire. Mentors help you stay on course. Success is guaranteed as long as you keep working on the goal.

Determination overcomes failure: What happens if you run into obstacles on the path to your goal? You push through or create a new path. That's the thing about determination; it helps you keep going regardless of what's in front of you. With determination, failure is just a diversion; it's not an end. The mistakes of yesterday should be lessons, not reasons for despair. Believe in yourself; you are in control of your life. Even in the most difficult moments, you still get to decide what to do. Believe in your ability to reach your goals.

If you're worried that you are not determined enough, you can take steps to improve your grit rather than give up. You can:

Stay focused on the future and let the past guide you, but never let it consume you.

Believe in your ability to reach your goals.

Celebrate others' success; you can achieve yours if you stay focused and positive.

Have smaller goals within a larger one; give yourself milestones, then focus on one mile at a time.

Be grateful for what you already have; that way you remain positive.

Link up with a mentor and people of like minds.

10 HABITS OF GREAT PEOPLE WITH DETERMINATION AND WILLPOWER

1. They derive value from their past – not liability.

The past is valuable. You need to learn from your mistakes and the mistakes of others; then let them go. The possibility of this depends on your perspective. When something bad happens to you, see it as an opportunity to learn something new. When another person makes a mistake, don't just learn from it – see it as an opportunity to be kind, forgiving, and understanding. The past is just training; it doesn't demean you. Think about what went wrong but only in terms of how you and the people around you will get it right the next time.

2. They see their life and future totally as within their control.

"Pray as if God will take care of all; act as if all is up to you." – Ignatius. While we commit everything to the hands of God, we need to get to work. God is in charge of the rain and bounty harvest, but you have to plant the seeds yourself. Many people think success or failure has to do with luck. If they succeed, it means luck favored them; and if they fail, luck was against them. Most successful people also think good luck played some role in their success. But they don't wait around for good luck or worry about bad luck. They act as if their success or failure is within their control. If they succeed, they caused it; if they fail, they caused it. Do not waste mental energy worrying about what might happen to you, instead, put all your efforts into making things happen. You can't control luck if it exists, but you can control what you do or not.

3. They learn to ignore the things they can't control.

When you have done all that is expected of you as you work towards success, certain things are naturally beyond your control, and here, you are to give them over to God. He deals with the impossible. In Moses's leadership experience, when the children of Israel got to the Red Sea, there was nothing else Moses could do for his followers, but their story didn't end there. They crossed! Mental strength is like muscle strength – no one has an unlimited supply. So why waste your power on things you can't control? It might be in politics, family, global warming, career; or whatever it is you care about and want others to care about as well. Do what you can do; vote, lend a listening ear, recycle and reduce your carbon footprint, etc. Be the change, but don't try to make everyone else change.

4. Those with determination genuinely celebrate the success of others.

Mentors are truly happy for whatever their protégés become, the same as other leaders and successful people. Haters often remain backward, and when they seem to succeed, they don't enjoy their success because they are alone. These people see success as a zero-sum game: there's only so much to go around. When someone else shines, they think that diminishes theirs. Resentment sucks up a massive amount of mental energy that is better applied elsewhere. When a friend does something awesome, that doesn't preclude you from doing something awesome as well or doing better. Where success is concerned, birds of a feather tend to flock together, so draw your successful friends closer. Learn to celebrate awesomeness in other people.

5. They remain positive and endeavour to communicate positivity.

You have great powers with your words, especially over your life and success. Whining about your problems will make you feel worse, not better. So if something is wrong, don't waste time complaining. Put that mental energy into making the situation better with whatever you have. If you can't do it on your own, get help. Why waste time? Get to work and fix it.

Don't talk about what's wrong; talk about how you'll make things better. You must carry an air of determination and positivity. Do the same around your friends, family and colleagues. Don't just serve as a shoulder they can cry on. Friends don't let friends whine; friends help friends make their lives better. Develop yourself into a solution and a beacon of hope.

6. They are self-motivated.

Rather than focusing on others, people with determination strive to impress themselves. No one likes you for your clothes, cars, possessions, title, or accomplishments. These are all things. People may like your things but that doesn't mean they like you. Genuine relationships make you happier, and that will only happen when you stop trying to impress and start being yourself. Some distractions will come in our interaction with others, and if care is not taken, they are capable of silencing your voice. But those that are determined to succeed make sure that they are heard, loud and clear. They give up mere compliments for a big congratulation. If people love you as much as they claim, they must help you succeed, but unfortunately, most people are only around you for what they can gain from you. So if you live your life trying to impress them, when will you start living for yourself?

7. They constantly keep their long-term goals in focus.

This enables you to develop a pattern until it becomes your routine. If you want to own or run a bank, you develop yourself as CEO and not as a teller, even if that's your current reality. Sometimes when you're mentally tired, it's easy to rationalize performing below par. Mental fatigue makes us take the easy way out, even though the easy way is the wrong way. The key is to create tangible reminders that will pull you back from the impulse brink. A friend has a copy of his bank note taped to his computer monitor as a constant reminder of an obligation he must meet. Another keeps a photo of himself, taken when he weighed 50 pounds more, on his refrigerator to serve as a constant reminder of the person he never wants to be again. Think of moments when you are most likely to give in to impulses that take you farther away from your long-term goals. Then use tangible reminders of those goals to interrupt the impulse and keep you on track. You can also rework your environment to eliminate your ability to be impulsive. This way, you don't have to exercise any willpower. If you can't say no to checking your social media accounts every few minutes, turn them off and put them away for a couple of hours. You don't have to be strong enough to say no.

8. They always count their blessings.

Most times, because of the size of your dream, you feel you are not making progress. You think that there is still a long way to go. Yes! But you can appreciate and approach the future courageously if you look back and recall how far you have come. Before you go to bed every day, take a moment to think of what you already have. Quit worrying about the other things you don't have; that way, you remain optimistic.

9. They stay connected.

It is not a sign of weakness to seek the support of others when you get stuck. Don't die trying to play a hero; the universe is there to support you. The earth covers about 510 million km3 surface area and has about 7.8 billion people in it, so there are enough glories to go around. Be a team player. Get a mentor or network of professional colleagues you can lean on and learn from to grow. Those with determination appreciate the power of networking. They know they cannot achieve everything on their own but still put in their best, and with the help of those around them, they reach their full potential.

10. They teach determination.

Successful mentees grow to become mentors themselves, and the cycle of building great leaders continues unabated. It is a known fact that you learn faster and better when you teach others. So those tested and successful methods you use to stay determined, that gave great results, teach others. Create an environment of determined minds!

You can begin your journey to greatness. The best way to advance is to keep the big goals in focus while putting effort into the small goals and daily tasks. Stay positive!

TRANSFORMING MENTORSHIP STORIES

#1

One of my unique experiences with career mentors began during my doctoral studies in 2010 when I won a prestigious European Union MycoRed Short Term Fellowship. I stayed at the International Institute of Tropical Agriculture (IITA) headquarters where I worked in the laboratory of Dr Ranajit Bandyopadhyay. Dr Ranajit was (and is still) indeed an excellent mentor; he was disciplined, encouraged hard work and was kind. He believed in me, taught me the standard manner of email communication, and manuscript writing and opened up avenues for me to enjoy collaboration with World Class Scientists in Europe. Dr Ranajit also gave me opportunities to grow by (a) offering me a 21-month stay (2012-2013) to lead a German Government funded project worth €60,000, (b) hiring me as a Consultant to support the setting up of a Regional Mycotoxin Testing Facility in Kenya, and (c) recommending me for the Technical Advisor position (16 months) at the Partnership for Aflatoxin Control in Africa of the African Union Commission at her headquarters in Addis Ababa.

Another mentor is Prof. Rudolf Krska; he is the best mentor any young scientist could have. He is a blessing from my 2010 MycoRed Fellowship. Prof. Krska is kind, compassionate, disciplined, encouraging, supportive, accessible and open. He recognized my strengths and provided enough avenues for me to develop them by offering me several postdoctoral stays in his World Class laboratory at the Institute of Bioanalytics and Agro-Metabolomics, Department of Agrobiotechnology, Austria. He recommended me as an invited speaker twice to the prestigious World Mycotoxin Forum held in Vienna and Amsterdam. Prof. Krska always gives me opportunities to grow.

PROF. CHIBUNDU N. EZEKIEL

Professor of Food Microbiology & Mycotoxicology, Babcock University, Nigeria

Scientific Staff/Researcher, Institute of Bioanalytics & Agro-Metabolomics, Austria.

#2

As a fresh graduate out of University and a "J.J.C" (newcomer) in the city of Abuja, I was greatly determined to succeed at every work I could venture into, I tried many hustles but there was so much still to learn. That's when my mentor, Bode, stepped in. Bode owned an Audit Firm and was an accomplished Chartered Accountant and Tax Consultant. But more than that, he was a kind and patient person who always made me feel like I was so much more than I saw myself at the time. He saw something in me that I hadn't seen yet, and he was determined to help me tap into it.

One day, Bode walked into the computer centre where I worked part-time (in the evenings) as a computer appreciation instructor. He needed someone to guide him through 2 voluminous manuals for the CISA examinations. The computer centre did not offer such courses nor support, but something inside of me saw this as a big opportunity, a chance to venture into a new line and also close in on a major client. He did not question my zeal but offered me the opportunity. He handed me the 2 manuals and I would read and study the modules during the day on my own while we will run through tutorials in the evening for 2 weeks ahead of his exams. I was both excited and terrified at the prospect, but Bode assured me that he had faith in my abilities to deliver on this. It was a tasking 2 weeks and to God's glory, Bode passed the CISA examinations in the end. After his success, I was invited over to his office and he said to me; "You seem like you have the head for numbers. Would you like to work for me?" You can figure out the rest.

Over the next 10 years, we worked closely together, bouncing ideas off each other, critiquing and refining work plans and designs, and pushing each other to be our best. It was a lot of hard work, but it was also an incredibly rewarding experience. I felt like I was finally starting to find my voice as a business solution provider, and I had Bode to thank for it.

Looking back right now brings back fond memories of how we loved our work, the commendations we received, as well as a lot of positive feedback from colleagues and clients. But for me, the real reward was the sense of accomplishment and confidence that I gained through the process. I realized that with the right guidance and support, I was capable of achieving things that I had never thought possible. I believe the same is true for everyone. That experience was a turning point for me. It showed me the value of mentorship and the power of having someone believe in you. And it's something that I'll always be grateful to Bode for.

SAM NWAOKOMAH

Business Solution Consultant. Abuja, Nigeria.

#3

Prof. Ezekiel is a goal-driven, caring and disciplined man who wants the best for his mentee. He is always driving me hard to step beyond my comfort zone and be the best version of myself. His academic footprints enabled me as a mentee to collaborate with the best in my chosen field. He is generous, and always ready to support research work with his own money. He always listens to me as we discuss research work and life issues. He has taught me the value of working as a team and the real definition of "a tree does not make a forest". His honesty, work ethic, and trustworthiness have shaped the kind of person I am in the field of academics.

OLUWAPELUMI OYEDELE

Doctoral Student and Faculty Member, Babcock University. Ilishan, Nigeria.

#4

I believe that having a mentor is one of the finest things that can happen to any young person. I grew up with several mentors in various aspects of my life. Largely, socializing with individuals older than me helped shaped my life decisions. Making a career choice is one of those critical moments you would realize that you need someone else with experience to guide you. My undergraduate study was a walk in the park since I understood what I wanted at the time and the path I should take; I only needed little input from external sources, but when it came to choosing a postgraduate program, I was stumped. Since the world is changing continuously, I must stay relevant and to pick a professional path that will help me do this, I had to turn to one of my mentors.

I presented my options to my mentor, Dr Raymond Okoro, which were either to continue as an economist or become a project manager. The second hurdle was choosing where to study. After several sessions of brainstorming, we considered global trends in technology especially the emerging stride with Artificial Intelligence (AI); project management had better prospects. To get the best exposure to opportunities and experiences, my mentor helped me choose the best school abroad. As the adage goes, "two good heads are better than one"; and I will include that it has to be an experienced head because having a good mentor, especially for young people like me should be non-negotiable, you just need the right guide to get along.

OTUONYE STELLA CHISOM,

Student. Northampton, United Kingdom.

I have known Professor Ezekiel for about 10 years. First, as my lecturer during my undergraduate program, and later as my supervisor and mentor. He is by far the best mentor any young researcher could ask for. He is highly disciplined, dedicated, intentional and kind.

Prof. Ezekiel has been very instrumental towards my career growth and development. In the past 5 years, I have acquired several skills through his teachings and mentorship especially, in the areas of grant and manuscript writing, project planning and execution, and research outputs. Furthermore, Prof. Ezekiel ensured that I attend several training, workshops and conferences that are useful to my career growth. Through his guidance, I have benefited from several fruitful collaborations with renowned scientists across Europe, the USA and Africa. Through such collaborations, I won a prestigious International Fellowship that enabled me to carry out the laboratory component of my PhD program at a reputable laboratory in Europe.

I consider Prof. Ezekiel to be a mentor and a friend. I am currently a Postdoctoral Fellow in a prestigious laboratory in Austria, where I work as an expert in the field of food safety and exposomics.

DR KOLAWOLE AYENI

Expert in Food Safety & Exposomics, Austria.

#6

The beauty of mentorship lies in the impact it has, both on the mentor and the mentee, anything less will not be a perfect exercise. I experienced the power of mentorship after meeting Nkasiobi Sabs-Mbonu, who had just finished Babcock university when she called to ask me to help her become a better poet. After brief introductions, the mentorship began as online sessions and progressed to physical meetings. Nkasi was humble and brilliant with an open mind to learning and relearning that which she already knew. She was very willing to take on daunting tasks that were way outside her comfort zone and soon, we started to record little successes.

When you ask me why this is one of my most unique, memorable and transforming mentorship experiences, I will tell you it is because of the amount of learning that went on both ways within the period and the transformations we have seen in our works as the years go by. Nkasi was instrumental in helping me with some of my award-winning projects at the time and years after, I am proud to say that she has so grown as a writer with books published in her name. I feel confident giving her my manuscripts to edit before I send them out. I believe my influence on her was so great that she has now grown to become a teacher and has continued to take younger ones under her wings, and the process of liberating minds has continued. This, for me, is a mentorship process that yielded the best fruit and why I always use it as a reference point for what great mentorship programs should look like.

SOONEST NATHANIEL,

Mentor, Author & Poet, Abuja, Nigeria.

#7

I live in Abeokuta, Nigeria and I worked as a safety manager in a manufacturing company where my salary was less than one hundred thousand naira (₦100,000). This could barely cater for my immediate family and me, so I continued to look for other sources of income. I was introduced to network marketing while combining it with my job. I must say life became more difficult. But things began to turn around for me when Mr Ola introduced himself and agreed to mentor me through his Omegapro network business in January 2020. My interest in the business grew when I started to earn extra income and saw his team thrive where other businesses were collapsing due to the impact of COVID-19. Mentorship has made a significant impact on my entire life as I am now a full-time entrepreneur, promoting the Omegapro business. I am grateful that my mentor introduced me to his mentor who was the National leader of the company at the time. Three to four hours training with Late Engr. Vincent Udoye unleashed the super recruiter I never knew existed in me.

By October 2020, after about 10 months of working full-time in my new career, I got to the third leadership rank in the company, went on an international trip with leaders, and gifted myself a new Toyota Corolla 2007 saloon car. I have continued to enjoy a good working relationship with my team leader/mentor and I am now a proud mentor of hundreds of other young entrepreneurs like me. Today, I am a six-figure earner on monthly basis, I drive my dream car, own properties, and run multiple businesses.

ADENIYI OPEYEMI,

Serial Entrepreneur, Abeokuta, Nigeria.

#8

My PhD supervisor and mentor, Prof Ezekiel C.N, has been a pleasure to work with. He did everything, from offering me advice and critique on scientific writing to assisting me in building my career and searching for post-doctoral opportunities, award-winning grant writing tutelage, and even attending seminars, conferences, and other events. He never failed to provide excellent guidance and encouraging support in my career and other aspects of my life. The most valuable lessons he taught me were the importance of consistency, patience, and tenacity. The finest part of my relationship with my mentor is knowing that someone is always rooting for me. It is nice to have someone who genuinely cares about my development and wants to see me succeed.

DR MUIZ O. AKINYEMI

Computer Biologist & Food Safety Analyst, South Africa

#9

Mentorship is a word that has added great value to me. It saves time and helps mould average people to become globally renowned when properly utilized. I had my first experience of mentorship when I started my entrepreneurial journey with an American company some years ago. Mr Afolabi Amos was a leader in the business, and his success story thrilled me, especially because of the unique way he coached team members and created a simple success roadmap for anyone to thrive. I was struggling with how to pay my dept of about $1000 at the time and also settle a pressing domestic need worth about $500. I shared with him how badly I needed a change and he helped me achieve all by simply teaching me how to use an action-based to-do list. I broke down my goals into daily plans and had a monthly savings target. It worked like magic and I was debt free within 3 months.

His mentorship equipped me with skills that saved me 10 years' worth of trial and error. I was able to achieve my immediate and short-term personal and business goals, a feat that other team members are still struggling to attain. This relationship has taught me, among other things, that "if you don't have a mentor, you will be tormented".

MAKANJUOLA EMMANUEL OLADAPO

Global Wealth Connector, Benin City, Nigeria.

ABOUT THE AUTHOR

David Chiemela Ogidinta is a widely read author and inspirational speaker, well known for his 'New Money' mantra, a digital value creator and entrepreneur, public health professional, youth leader and mentor.

David started his mentorship career in 2009 at Babcock University where he assembled an army of young people of like minds called ALABASTER to carry on the campaign of personal and influential leadership which was launched with a 13-week self-discovery series on the university radio. He is the author of the book, Eagle Mind; how to discover and lead your mind to its full potential.

He holds a master's degree in public health and volunteers for many local and international NGOs. An educator and entrepreneur with a global network of about three thousand people. This book Mentored will tell you more about the author.

www.ingramcontent.com/pod-product-compliance
Lightning Source LLC
Chambersburg PA
CBHW050330220526
45465CB00012B/436